Finding the BEST
and the BRIGHTEST

Finding the BEST
and the BRIGHTEST

☆ ☆ ☆ ☆ ☆

A guide to recruiting, selecting, and retaining effective leaders

PEG THOMS

Westport, Connecticut
London

Library of Congress Cataloging-in-Publication Data

Thoms, Peg, 1948–
    Finding the best and the brightest : a guide to recruiting, selecting, and
    retaining effective leaders / Peg A. Thoms.
        p.   cm.
    Includes bibliographical references and index.
    ISBN 0-275-98411-7 (alk. paper)
    1. Executives—Recruiting.   2. Employee selection.   3. Employee retention.
    4. Leadership.   I. Title.
    HF5549.5.R44T465 2005
    658. 4'07111—dc22   2005013507

British Library Cataloguing in Publication Data is available.

Library of Congress Catalog Card Number: 2005013507
ISBN: 0-275-98411-7

First published in 2005

Praeger Publishers, 88 Post Road West, Westport, CT 06881
An imprint of Greenwood Publishing Group, Inc.
www.praeger.com

Printed in the United States of America

The paper used in this book complies with the
Permanent Paper Standard issued by the National
Information Standards Organization (Z39.48-1984).

10   9   8   7   6   5   4   3   2   1

This book is dedicated to Myke and Dave,
the best and the brightest.

Contents

	Acknowledgments	ix
1	The Selection of Leaders Matters	1
2	What We Know about Effective Leaders	9
3	Identifying Necessary Leader Attributes	21
4	Recruiting Leaders	43
5	Leadership Selection Tools	55
6	Developing and Conducting a Structured Interview	67
7	Structured Interview Questions	77
8	Putting the Pieces Together	111
9	Developing Leaders to Fit the Organization	125
10	Retaining Effective Leaders	139
11	Selecting Government Leaders	159
12	Improving Organizations through Improved Leadership	169
	Notes	175
	Index	177

Acknowledgments

Thank you to Nicholas Philipson for assistance and support. Thank you to Christina L. Quick for proofreading and suggestions on a draft of this book.

The Selection of Leaders Matters

We all choose our leaders. Each and every one of us is involved in the selection of leaders, either directly or indirectly, in all aspects of our lives. We hire them. We accept jobs under them. We vote for them. We follow them. Many of us make decisions about whom to hire for leadership positions in our organizations. We conduct interviews with candidates, observe them during the selection process, and provide input on which applicant to select. Any time we accept a job, we are choosing a leader. We have been interviewed, have had the opportunity to gather information about the leader and the organization, and have decided which leader we want to work for. We listen to political candidates' speeches, read and listen to expert commentary about them, and cast ballots for the leaders we choose. Or we do not vote and allow others to choose leaders for us. Either way, we choose. Leaders are only leaders if someone follows them. By taking direction, going to bat or war, following orders, marching behind, listening, and agreeing, we are choosing to allow another individual to lead us.

Effective leaders matter. Strong leaders make a significant difference to the people that they lead. Choosing the right person to lead a department, division, company, or country can have many consequences, which may result in improved profitability, repeat customers, happier and healthier employees or members, and even world peace, depending on the level of leadership and the type of organization or group. Choosing the wrong person to lead a department, division, company, or country can have disastrous consequences, including lawsuits, layoffs, bad publicity, and even violence.

Most people believe that they know a great leader when they see one. Despite this belief, we continue to choose, hire, and elect poor leaders. Although it may be true that most of us know an effective leader when we see one, that knowledge comes after the fact. In other words, we usually do not know what we are getting until it is too late.

Virtually all recent literature on the subject of leadership has focused on transformational leadership. This is a problem for two reasons. First, we do not know how to identify transformational leaders before we pick them. Common perceptions and judgments about which people are likely to be transformational are typically based on brief interactions and a public persona, which can be very misleading. In addition, it is a myth that the ideal leader for every organization must be a visionary born to transform. In reality, the type of leader needed depends on the situation. Present-oriented leaders who focus on current issues are much more effective in building customer relations, solving problems, and streamlining day-to-day operations. On the other hand, transformational leaders can be very effective in dynamic industries during periods of change when innovation is necessary.

The key to finding and selecting the type of leader that an organization requires is a thorough assessment of the organization. For example, the following questions must be answered before we can decide what kind of leader we need:

- What is presently occurring in our organization or community that requires leadership?
- What is happening in our industry? What are the trends?
- What problems do we face?
- What types of leaders do we already have? What types of leaders are we missing?
- What traits and behaviors do we need in a leader?

The first step in selecting a leader is an assessment of the organizational situation. What events, trends, activities, and people must be considered to determine the leadership needs? In other words, what is happening? Has a company's product been copied and marketed by foreign competitors? Does the company have to find a way to differentiate its products?

Is the country where the company is headquartered in a recession, meaning that the company needs a leader who can influence economic variables? Does the city have a high unemployment rate and need to attract new employers? Is the organization enjoying increased growth in sales that it would like to maintain when replacing the outgoing sales manager? Has the coach of a successful team decided to leave after a winning season, and the school district has to find a comparable coach? Has the founder of a public company with decreasing market share decided to retire without a successor who has been adequately trained to take over? Each of these situations is unique and requires a different type of leader.

To illustrate this point, here are examples of the types of leaders needed in each of the preceding situations:

Example 1. A company's product been copied and marketed by foreign competitors and the company must find a way to differentiate its products.

The leader must understand global business and international business law, be capable of conducting and understanding a complex product market analysis, have research and development experience in a comparable industry, be future oriented, and have done advanced coursework in marketing and international business.

Example 2. The country where the company is headquartered is in a recession, meaning that the company needs a leader who can influence economic variables.

The leader must have a strong grounding in economic theory and development through graduate coursework, be well connected to the finance and business sectors of government and industry, have a thorough understanding of government's impact on the economy, have very effective working relationships with elected representatives, be present oriented, and have strong links to international economic players.

Example 3. The city has a high unemployment rate and a Rust Belt industry with declining sales, and must attract new employers.

The leader should have a good understanding of state and national funding sources, be knowledgeable about entrepreneurship, have links to local businesses, be future oriented, and have excellent sales and public relations skills.

Example 4. The company is enjoying increased growth that it would like to maintain when replacing the outgoing sales manager.

The leader should be an in-house manager or lead sales person with experience in both sales and marketing, have strong communications skills, have positive relationships with all major customers, have a personal interest in the company and the community, have some understanding of operations, and be goal oriented.

Example 5. A local school district must find a coach to take over a winning program.

The leader should have a reputation for coaching either at the assistant or head coach level in the area around the community; extensive experience coaching the sport; positive relationships with his or her current school officials, school board, players, and parents; extensive knowledge of safety and athletic training; a willingness to wait and gradually make changes to the current program; and a positive attitude toward children, life, and the game.

Example 6. A public company that has seen decreasing market share must replace a founder who decided to retire.

The leader must be experienced with the type of product produced and sold by the company, should hold an MBA, and must have business leadership experience in successful organizations, excellent communications skills, and a complex vision of the future of the organization.

Once the basic skill set has been identified, one of the biggest problems in selecting effective leaders is not aggressively recruiting them. The tendency is to hire from a pool of candidates who want the job. In other words, they have selected themselves as candidates for the position. More aggressive recruiting of qualified applicants would improve the quality of leadership in our organizations. Another major pitfall is using only an interview or a series of interviews to select leaders. Several other tools can and should be used to make better decisions when hiring for leadership positions.

The primary purpose of this book is to help readers learn how to identify the types of leaders and the traits and behaviors that are best suited for different situations. Then the book provides guidance on how to recruit and select the proper candidate for leadership positions. Such positions may include chairs of committees, presidents of social clubs, managers of departments or divisions, elected officials, board members of religious organizations, management trainees, or even the CEO of a corporation. Readers will learn to develop, list, and describe the skills and traits required for the leadership position being filled. They will also learn to select and use a variety of recruiting strategies to find and attract people with the appropriate skills, thereby creating a pool of qualified candidates. Readers are given a detailed description of selection tools they can use to help match candidates to leadership positions. In addition, guidance is provided on the development and retention of effective leaders.

Throughout the book, examples are provided of how six different organizations could recruit and hire leaders for their specific situations. These examples range from a small special-interest club looking for a president to a large city hospital that needs a CEO. The examples include specific strategies for recruiting, selecting, and retaining effective leaders.

Using a more effective approach to the selection of leaders seems to be a win-win proposition, but in many organizations, implementing more effective approaches is met with resistance. Why would anyone be opposed to improving the quality of leaders? Most people are naturally resistant to change and prefer the systems currently used for selecting leaders. Some of these people have received promotions in the past because they play political games well, have influential (or wealthy) mentors or backers, fit the stereotypical profile preferred by decision makers, are willing to do whatever it takes to get a leadership position, or inherit leadership roles because they are related to the owner. Others prefer the current selection systems because they benefit in other ways from using traditional approaches to selecting leaders. A superficial review of business, economic, and political news over the past ten years is proof that poor leadership may provide advantages to some customers, constituents, and followers.

Why bother? Applying strategic selection tools can increase the effectiveness of leadership in every organization, from small social clubs to national professional organizations, from small towns to large cities, from counties to countries, from mom-and-pop stores to multinational corporations, from small liberal arts colleges to large public land-grant universities, and from high school teams to professional clubs. Measures of effectiveness include winning teams, increasing profits, and effectively competing with foreign companies. The measure of success is another variable that must be considered when choosing leaders. Selecting the right leader for specific jobs works because it increases leaders' accountability, improves their chances of success, and provides specific direction as to what organizational members and followers find important.

Too often, people discover that they are not going to be promoted to leadership at their current organization, and they give up. They might mistakenly assume that they are not leadership material. This belief is based on the false assumption that all leaders, regardless of the situation in which they find themselves, need the same traits and characteristics. In reality, many very effective community leaders may have failed in business or other endeavors. The key is finding the right organization where one's talents and skills can be most effectively used.

There are advantages for both organizations and leaders in improving the selection process. Organizations will have better leaders and leaders will be more successful. It sounds like common sense. So why is it not done now?

For one thing, few people understand how to identify the traits needed for specific situations and how to recruit and choose the right leader. The reason people do not know how to select leaders is that there are gaps in the leadership literature, which has a superficial slant toward situational issues of leadership. Current leadership training assumes that anyone can become a leader, and promotes naive myths which imply that all effective leaders share the same traits and behaviors. Who emerges as the best and brightest can only be determined by examining the possibilities through a situational lens.

The other problem is that we all look for easy answers. We do not like to do the difficult and time-consuming work that a good selection process involves. The political ads for presidential campaigns are an excellent example. We gather most of our information about whom to elect to the most important leadership position in the United States from biased sound bites that distort facts. Few of us conduct our own research to make an informed decision. We rely on stereotypes about what kind of person makes the best president, our party affiliations, or superficial distinctions like physical appearance and observable behavior in staged and televised public forums. Why? We do it because it is easier than doing the homework ourselves. If we take shortcuts when choosing the president, will we also take shortcuts when choosing leaders for the smaller organizations of which we are all members? We do it every day.

Seeking mental shortcuts is human and natural. Our minds are constantly following the stream. We only stop and rethink our approach to selecting leaders when something grabs our attention. For example, if we have lost our jobs or our son or daughter is sent to war or we lose a loved one in a terrorist attack, then we will pay closer attention to the candidates and what they say and do. If we find that another company has taken market share, we begin to look at our CEO and executives with new eyes. If our community center has scheduling problems, we may spend more time hiring the next director.

For purposes of clarity, it is necessary to distinguish between leaders and managers, and this distinction is used throughout the book. On the cover of their book, Bennis and Nanus described the difference this way: "Managers do things right. Leaders do the right thing."[1] Their definition covers both the fact that leaders get things done and that they make good choices. It does not, on the other hand, exaggerate the impact of effective leaders, as many other authors, leadership experts, and leaders do. We do not need to exaggerate the importance of leadership by inferring magical or mystical properties. Doing the right thing is both important and rare.

What We Know about Effective Leaders

This was the most difficult chapter of this book to write. How does one summarize thousands of pages of research articles, hundreds of books, and decades of research on a subject as intangible as leadership? This problem is magnified when much of that research has produced inconclusive and even contradictory findings. This may explain why most experts believe that the quality of leadership has not improved despite intense examination.[1] In addition, some of the leaders who appear to have had the most important and dramatic impact on their followers, as well as the rest of us, are negative examples. No attempt is made here to adequately describe the range and depth of leadership theories that have been written and research that has been conducted. Instead, I provide a basic overview of leadership traits and behaviors that have been found to correlate, in some situations, with effective leadership. This provides a starting point for understanding and improving the selection of leaders.

Historically, leadership theories have fallen into two categories: universal or contingency (often called situational) theories. Universal theories suggest that there are traits and behaviors that are shared by all effective leaders. Situational theories suggest that different situations require different leadership traits and behavior by leaders. Much of the research on leadership has shown that no single theory completely explains the effectiveness of good leaders. (For a good review of the research on leadership, see Yukl.[2]) Of course, how effectiveness is measured is a major controversy in the leadership field too. Should we attempt to measure a leader's influence on the lives of followers? If so, how are intangible feelings and attitudes toward leaders measured? Should we examine bottom-line measures like profitability or unemployment rates or the number of wars fought and won? Researchers have not been able to agree on this, so the dilemma of how to measure leadership effectiveness has made studying leadership very difficult. This chapter provides a list of the traits and behaviors that have been identified by leadership experts as the most desirable for good leaders. This information is provided, however, with the caveat that the research is inconclusive.

Traits of Good Leaders

One of the best-known leadership researchers in the twentieth century was Stogdill. In 1974, he reviewed 163 trait studies and found that successful leaders were characterized by the following traits:[3]

- Strong drive for responsibility and task completion
- Vigor and persistence in accomplishment of goals
- Adventurousness and originality in problem solving
- Drive to exercise initiative in social situations
- Self-confidence
- Sense of personal identity
- Willingness to accept consequences of decisions and actions
- Readiness to accept interpersonal stress
- Tolerance for frustration and delay
- Ability to influence other people's behavior
- Capacity to structure social interactions to achieve goals

Stogdill was careful to suggest that having these traits was not a guarantee of effective leadership. As he clearly stated, the impact of a trait on leadership effectiveness depends on the situation. A tolerance for frustration and delay may well serve a city manager who is waiting for a government contract to be signed, but will not be particularly useful to a CEO with an R & D staff that is dragging its feet on the testing of a new product scheduled for release next month. In other words, the situation determines which traits are most useful and will bring desired results.

In a book published in 1985, McClelland summarized twenty years of research on managerial motivation.[4] He and others found that the most successful managers in large organizations have a moderately high need for achievement, a relatively low need for affiliation, and a strong socialized power orientation. However, they found that owner-managers of small businesses do best if they have a high need for achievement.

People with a high need for achievement enjoy accomplishing difficult tasks, meeting standards and goals, and performing on their own. People with a high need for affiliation want to be liked and accepted by others, and they tend to be friendly and cooperative. People with a high need for power like to exercise influence over other people. However, McClelland has found that expertise in the field of business is critical to the success of any enterprise, so managerial motivation is only one indicator of possible success.

Bass has studied leaders and their behavior for many years.[5] He and other researchers have identified a number of traits that have been found to be related to effective leadership, including the following:

- *Energy level and stress tolerance*—a high level of physical energy and an ability to handle stressful situations well, both coupled with good health[6]
- *Emotional stability*—well adjusted, no psychological illnesses, not neurotic
- *Integrity*—honest, behaves in ways consistent with personal values and those shared with followers[7]
- *Strong interpersonal skills*—communicates well with others in one-on-one situations and in social settings
- *Technical skills*—has the appropriate skills for the job, whether they are engineering skills, accounting skills, human resources skills, computer skills, or some other skill
- *Cognitive skills*—has the mental skills required for the position, which may include high general intelligence, analytical ability, and so on.
- *Self-confidence*—belief in one's ability to succeed as a leader of a group
- *Internal locus of control*—belief that one has control over what happens[8]

Yukl points out that most research on traits of effective leaders has used analysis that examines simple linear relationships.[9] For example, as emotional stability goes up, measures of leadership performance also go up. Unfortunately, this does not allow for variations in organizations, jobs, tasks, and level of the leader in the organization. The point is that emotional stability, like all of the other traits, is going to be more important in certain situations than in others.

Behaviors of Good Leaders

The same can be said about leader behavior—the leader behavior that results in increased performance in one setting may not have that effect in another. Nonetheless, researchers have identified a number of behaviors that are associated with results. In the 1950s and 1960s, a series of studies were done that identified two basic categories of leader behavior:[10]

- *Consideration behavior*—providing support and encouragement to followers or subordinates, being friendly and helpful
- *Initiating structure behavior*—organizing the work and the responsibilities of members of the organization, setting standards and goals, providing feedback, problem solving

During the same period, a second series of studies examined similar leader behaviors, including these:[11]

- *Task-oriented behavior*—planning and scheduling work, coordinating assignments, providing resources as needed, guiding the work of subordinates
- *Relations-oriented behavior*—providing support and encouragement to followers or subordinates, developing others, providing necessary information
- *Participative leadership behavior*—guiding the work and performance of others and supervising the group as a whole, providing support to those doing the day-to-day tasks of the unit

Although most would agree that managers are different from leaders, some experts have developed lists of managerial behavior that include items like planning, delegating, and rewarding. These behaviors are the technical skills needed to manage others, particularly in formal organizations where there are norms for the behavior of everyone. Certainly such behaviors are important in many situations, but they may not be required of all, or even most, leaders. When they are needed, an effective leader may have others in the organization who perform some or all of the managerial duties. For example, planning is typically done by members of a planning department in a large organization.

These management behaviors can be broken down into very specific types of things that a manager can practice doing. For example, coaching behavior may include activities like providing feedback, making suggestions for improving performance, and providing opportunities to practice skills.[12] In addition, some research on participative leadership has broken down different levels of subordinate involvement. This research provided very specific guidance to leaders who wanted to use a participative approach.[13]

Other research has identified behaviors common to transformational leaders. Transformational leadership theories tend to emphasize behavior that elicits emotional responses from followers. They distinguish between transactional influence, which provides rewards for specific follower behavior, and transformational influence, which creates high performance through motivation. For example, some of the behaviors typical of transformational leaders include the following:[14]

- *Idealized influence*—arousing follower emotions and commitment to the leader
- *Individualized consideration*—supporting, coaching, and encouraging followers
- *Inspirational motivation*—creating and communicating a vision of a better future
- *Intellectual stimulation*—changing followers' perspectives on issues to include creative approaches to problems and ownership

Other transformational leadership theories include similar behavior. Some are very specific about what leaders can do to become more effective (see Kouzes and Posner for an example).[15]

In my interviews with leaders ranging from college leaders to business CEOs, I have found that most began influencing others while they were young children. Many can remember specific events in their childhood when they were leading others at the age of four to five years. Either they liked being in charge and simply took over activities, or they were drafted by other children who saw something that made them more acceptable or desirable as leaders than others. Sometimes they were encouraged by parents who were leaders (and may have transferred the leadership genetic code to their children) to take leadership roles. Sometimes their parents did not encourage them and may even have tried to prevent their development as leaders by telling them to stop being so bossy.

Like many experts on personality, I believe humans are born with certain personality tendencies that are shaped into acceptable behavior by their culture and experience. People whose personalities do not allow adaptation to society either leave or are removed. Our personalities make us more interested in certain professional endeavors and social activities. Our personalities play a role in the development of skills and abilities, which we use to make a living doing what suits us. By the same token, some are born to lead and emerge as strong and effective leaders when they find themselves in the right settings and situations. Others with leadership personalities never find the right setting for their leadership potential and may suffer a high level of frustration watching others lead poorly. Others, who have no inclination to lead, spend their lives quite happily following.

Leadership training and education cannot do much to change these basic tendencies except to provide opportunities to practice leading. Opportunities to lead in classroom exercises and in work settings as part of a development program provide feedback on leader behavior. The feedback may be verbal and come from followers, trainers, or professors, or it may be quantitative and come from performance measures. The behavior can then be revised to become more acceptable to superiors, customers, and followers. It can also be modified to produce the level of performance necessary in a particular setting.

Situational Variables That Affect Leaders

Appropriate traits and behaviors vary depending on the situation. A number of situational variables might be used to determine which candidate and which behavior are best.

It needs to be understood from the outset that we cannot develop formal guidelines on how to select a leader based on the situation any more than we can develop definite guidelines for the selection of leaders based on traits and skills. For example, one of the most important situational considerations is the level of the leadership position. It seems obvious that a CEO needs different traits and skills than a first-line supervisor. Unfortunately, even this seemingly easy distinction is not quite so clear.

A CEO must have strategic planning skills. A first-line supervisor does not. What is not so obvious is that a CEO needs some of the same traits as a first-line supervisor and a first-line supervisor must have some of the same traits as a CEO. For example, both must have high integrity. We can never create a list of effective leader traits for CEOs and categorically say that other leaders who report to the CEO do not need them. Nor can we say that all CEOs need these traits in every organization. It depends on the specifics of the situation.

Besides the leader's level in the organization, other situational variables influence the type of leader needed. The skill levels of followers are important variables. Some researchers have noted that some followers have enough expertise and experience that they do not always need a leader to manage and coordinate their work.[16] Instead, they may only need support and recognition for their efforts. In addition, this theory suggests that organizational characteristics like cohesiveness among work groups, formality and flexibility of policies and procedures, and the presence of remote versus central work locations will also influence the type of leadership necessary.

The multiple-linkage model suggests that a number of complicated situational variables will determine the type of leadership needed.[17] Some of these situations include the type of work being performed, the amount of change in the environment, the number of tasks, dependency on supply sources, and interdependence with other units. For example, in a situation where the tasks are highly technical and complex and the work depends on another department, the leader must have a high level of technical skill and must have an excellent relationship with the other department.

There has yet to be a theory that adequately explains the complexity of leadership. Although leaders, followers, and researchers have searched for thousands of years for the keys to becoming and selecting the best leaders, the search has been futile. The intricate balance between individual traits, skills, and attitudes and the variety of situations in which leaders might find themselves render it virtually impossible to develop a theory that can predict what will make a person a great leader.

Here are some of the many aspects of an organization, with examples of just a few of the varieties in which they occur, that must be considered when selecting leaders:

- *Size of the organization*

  Corner store or multinational corporation

  Local private elementary school or public school district

  Local ski club or chain of ski resorts

  Rural community church or all of the churches in a region

  Franchise or corporate office of a large chain

- *Type of organization*

  For-profit business

  Not-for-profit social service agency

  Government agency

  Educational institution

  R & D operation

  Military

  Social club

- *Category within type of organization*

  Retail, manufacturing, financial, transportation, or recreational business enterprise

  Elementary school or college

  Township administration or federal government post

  Law practice or accounting firm

- *Problems common to all organizations*

  Poor economy

  Increased global competition

Weak dollar

Corporate and government scandals leading to distrust of all leaders

- *Specific problems*

  Lawsuits

  Located in a region with poor education

  High absenteeism and turnover

  Outdated technology

  Global competition for specific market

  Poor weather conditions

  Poverty in region

  Funding sources cut

  Changes in industry

  Poor work performance

- *Rate of change*

  Rapid, dynamic change in industry

  Stable environment

- *Organizational age*

  New clothing store at a new mall

  Fifty-year-old fraternity

  Thirty-five-year-old social service agency

  High-tech company started five years ago

  The Roman Catholic Church

  Luxury hotel with emphasis on service and tradition

- *Organizational culture*

  Formal, structured traditional organization (Bank One)

  Informal, unstructured social group (a private book club)

  Fast-paced (Microsoft)

Easygoing (Bible study group)

Masculine culture (General Electric)

Feminine culture (Mary Kay Cosmetics)

- *Mission*

To save the world

To save our souls

To help children learn basic skills

To make money

To make money however we can

To serve the community

To have fun

To create jobs

To find the truth

To seek justice

To put out fires

To keep citizens safe

- *Quality of followers*

Intelligence

Technical competency

Motivation to meet goals of the organization

Skill level

Ability to perform and produce

Integrity

- *Organizational needs*

Growth

Reduction in staffing

Improvement of reputation

Maintenance of reputation

Cost reduction

Updating of technology

How do you decide which candidate is best? How do you decide whom to hire, whom to vote for, whom to ask to take over, whom to follow? We must make those decisions by carefully analyzing each separately, one situation at a time, and then finding the person who has the attributes required by the specific situation. The common stereotype of the effective leader—the fast-paced attractive visionary with an MBA—works sometimes. Other times, it does not. We must look beyond our biases about who is the best and brightest to find the most effective leader who can help us meet our needs and our goals.

An effective leader will have values consistent with those of followers and other constituents, meet the goals of the followers, produce results for stockholders and stakeholders, model appropriate behavior for others in the organization, and genuinely care about the organization and its members. Each organization will have specific behaviors and objectives that must be met. Each job has specific tasks that must be completed. An effective leader will perform according to organizational requirements while making sure that the organization is operating within acceptable community standards.

The next chapter focuses on how to do an organizational assessment in order to identify the traits necessary to lead well. I present a variety of different situations and help explain how to identify desirable leader traits, skills, and attitudes.

3

Identifying Necessary Leader Attributes

The Manager Search

Let me describe a company in northwestern Pennsylvania. It is a small manufacturing company that provides parts for one Fortune 500 buyer and a few small companies. It employs approximately 450 workers, most in production jobs. This is the major employer in the small town where it is located. The large buyer has asked for repeated upgrades in the products it buys and has also asked for price reductions several times in the past five years. The buyer is continuously shopping the parts out to manufacturers in China in hopes of finding a cheaper supplier. A great deal of business in this industry is going to foreign manufacturers that have cheaper resources, lower production costs, and fewer government regulations.

Jim, the CEO, is the son of the founder. He has an engineering degree. He has attended numerous seminars on business topics, but has not earned an MBA. Jim knows his business very well, having worked there since he was fifteen, rotating among many of the departments. Jim is very wealthy, lives well, and is known in the community as a philanthropist. He has three children working in professional jobs in the organization (one doing well, one doing poorly, the third an average worker). All five of his children expect to run, if not own, the company within the next ten years. Jim does not know this.

Jim feels responsible for the welfare and employment of the 450 employees. He feels responsible for ensuring the future of the organization that his father started. He feels responsible toward the community where he grew up and raised his own children. Although he also feels responsible toward his children, he knows that none of them are capable of running the business effectively when he retires. Unfortunately, he has done all of his succession planning with his oldest son. He must identify and begin developing a new general manager who can manage the organization within five to ten years. He knows that if he does not accomplish this goal and something happens to him, the company will fold quickly.

What kind of leader does Jim need to find? Typically, we go one of two ways when we are looking for a leader. We can recruit people with the technical skills necessary and assume that a smart person can learn the management aspects. (After all, how hard is that?) Or we look for a dynamic, articulate visionary and assume that a smart person can learn the technical aspects. (After all, how hard is that?)

Unfortunately, we make more mistakes than just these two. We often assume that success in one business translates into success in another. For example, we may assume that someone who was effective at managing an insurance company can also manage a metal fabrications plant. Sometimes that is true, but often it is not. Or we assume that if a leader worked in a slightly different type of business (like plastics pulltrusions making truck caps) that he could never learn our specific business (like plastics extrusion molding of recycling bins). Sometimes that is true, but often it is not.

However, the most common mistake made in hiring managers in general, and leaders in particular, is choosing people who remind us of ourselves. This is not just a question of ego, thinking that people like us are better. Some might argue that point and discriminate on the basis that people who are not like us are not as good. Actually, it has much more to do with picking people who make us feel comfortable when we are around them. Life is easier when we deal with people on a regular basis who look and think like us. For instance, when a woman enters a "man's world," men worry about the language they use, the things they talk about, and a woman's perception of the things they do. It is not much fun for either the men or the woman.

Gender differences are an extreme example, but the same thing happens when educational levels, personalities, and personal interests are different between men. If Jim has an undergraduate degree in engineering from Purdue, lives in the small town where he grew up, is married with five children, and enjoys fishing, he will most likely feel uncomfortable around Tom, a man with an MBA from Harvard, who lives in Los Angeles, is single, and enjoys the theater. Regardless of his qualifications, Jim is very unlikely to hire Tom. His gut feeling will be negative. He will not be able to explain it. He will tell others, "I don't know why, but I just didn't feel good about the guy." In actuality, Tom could be the perfect general manager for the company—but we will never know.

To find the right leader, Jim must carefully list the traits, skills, and attitudes necessary to be successful in the job and then find the person who has the right attributes. He has to get past his gut feelings, appearances, and his intuition—right up until he has two equally qualified candidates. Then, and only then, does his personal comfort level become an appropriate criterion for selection. This issue is addressed further in later chapters.

Given this situation, what attributes should the new general manager have? Among other things, Jim must identify a person with the following traits, skills, and attitudes.

- *Expertise in manufacturing*—preferably with an industry leader. This company is competing with other manufacturing companies. The general manager will have to find ways to cut costs while retaining quality.
- *Well-rounded background in business*—preferably having earned an MBA and having at least fifteen to twenty years' experience in various capacities in comparable companies. Because the general manager is being groomed to become the CEO, running the entire organization, the person must have a broad background in business.
- A *quick learner*—someone who can come up to speed easily in order to understand the business and the industry. If this is not an internal manager, the general manager must learn everything about the company and the industry niche within the next six to twelve months.
- A *person with presence*—an individual who is noticed when entering a room and who inspires respect. This individual must sell the company and its products, convince buyers to stick with the company, and inspire employees.

- A *good communicator*—interacts well with individuals and groups, makes professional presentations, conducts effective meetings, and connects with community leaders. The general manager must provide and gather information on a continuous basis and build strong relationships in the organization, industry, and community.
- A *salesperson*—a person who can influence others and sell ideas, as well as products. The general manager will be the major spokesperson for the company and must visit the largest buyer and potential customers with the sales staff.
- A *self-starter*—a person who does not wait for direction. Jim cannot develop the general manager himself. He must hire someone who will identify the right strategies for learning the business and do it. He must hire a leader who shows initiative in everything that needs to be done.
- A *people person*—someone who enjoys interacting with others. To lead an organization, the general manager must enjoy daily interactions with others.
- An *optimist*—an individual who approaches every situation believing that he and others are capable of dealing with it, who has a generally positive attitude about life. Research indicates that optimistic people are more successful business leaders. A general manager must believe in his or her own ability and the abilities of followers.
- An *analyst*—someone who can read data and understand where problems exist, dissect important issues, and develop complex strategies and solutions. Running even a small company requires excellent analytical skills.
- A *person who can do multiple tasks in short time frames*—an individual who can review an advertising brochure and work on a corporate budget fifteen minutes later. A general manager, and later a CEO, is responsible for every aspect of the business and must be able to switch gears frequently throughout the day.
- An *intelligent person*—a new general manager must be intelligent in order to learn all that is required.
- A *person with a pleasant appearance, personality, and demeanor*—good looks are not required for this job, but a clean and neat appearance and a pleasant manner will help create productive relationships.
- A *person who will make a long-term commitment to the company*—this general manager is being groomed for the CEO position. The future

of the company depends on it. The new general manager must commit to staying with the company.

Once the right attributes have been identified, Jim can begin an intelligent search to find the right applicants and select the most effective leader for this job. He can improve the chances of hiring the best person and ensuring the future of the organization.

Identifying Leadership Attributes

Right now, we will practice identifying appropriate attributes for other situations. Six different scenarios are presented. Fill in the blanks after each. When you are done, compare your answers with the list provided at the end of the scenarios. Note that you will be asked to list attributes in various categories including personality, technical skills, management or leadership experience, and special abilities, traits, and characteristics. To determine the appropriate attributes, you must think about the desired outcomes. What does each organization need to accomplish through its leader? Does the leader need to develop a plan, raise money, handle finances, solve problems, and so on? Once you have identified the primary objectives that the leader must achieve, you will be better able to identify the attributes necessary.

You may need some ideas in each of the categories to help you match attributes with each scenario. The following lists include some attributes that might be appropriate in different situations, which may be helpful when completing the exercise. Do not say that every leader needs every one of the attributes listed. Remember that the perfect leader does not exist—let alone six of them. Pick only the attributes most appropriate for each of the scenarios. These are only partial lists. Add other attributes that seem right to you.

Personality

Authentic—this means that an individual has a strong sense of self, understands his or her strengths and weaknesses, and represents himself or herself accurately. What you see is what you get. This is particularly useful when a leader is expected to take a public position on issues.

Calm—valuable when the leader will be constantly dealing with emergencies and must project a controlled image to the public and not overreact to events.

Conscientious—a valuable trait in any position of authority.

Cooperative—particularly useful if the work of the organization depends on people and companies outside the organization.

Emotionally stable—important if a high level of stress is part of the position and others around the leader will experience a high level of stress.

Extroverted—helpful when the leader will have to interact regularly with others, both inside and outside the organization.

Friendly—needed by leaders who must work through and with others to accomplish the work of the organization.

High energy level—important if the leader must be continuously active at various tasks.

Honest—valuable in most situations, but especially when the leadership role involves handling money, dealing with children, and responsibility for the health and welfare of people in the community.

Optimistic—important when the leader must motivate or influence others, when facing difficult situations, and when the leader must create something new.

Pessimistic—valuable when the leader must anticipate and expect people to cheat or steal. For example, some attorneys and accountants need to be pessimistic to be most effective.

Salty—a person who is positive and open, but not naive. This attribute is important when a leader will face people who will lie or try to get away with inappropriate behavior, although they may not be malicious and must be handled carefully.

Technical Skills

Ability to influence others—most leaders must be able to sell ideas and products. This is especially useful in sales and marketing or in work groups that develop and pitch ideas to the rest of an organization.

Broad business knowledge—an MBA or an undergraduate degree in business from a high-quality university is critical for business executives who must deal with a cross section of business problems and issues. This skill is important from the level of director and up in staff positions and vice president and up in line positions.

Computer skills—the level of computer skills necessary will vary by the position. A vice president of information systems will be expected to know everything. A CEO may not need any computer skills. A first-line supervisor in a software development company may need leading-edge skills on a variety of software.

Engineering skills—the vice president of engineering for a large manufacturer of locomotives must be current in engineering techniques. In most situations, however, this is a problem because engineers' skills are out of date within months of graduation, yet promotions come after time in a job and an organization. In these cases, engineers who want to move into executive positions must spend a great deal of time making sure they have kept up with new knowledge in their fields.

Expertise in a specific field or industry—although this appears to be obvious, it really is not true for all leadership positions. Make sure that you need the specific expertise before narrowing down the candidate search. For example, school principals must be state certified, but an insurance training manager does not have to hold an insurance industry designation to conduct management and communications training.

Knowledge of the law—as it relates to the field or industry.

Language—Spanish would be critical for a vice president of global marketing whose primary market is Central and South America and who spends 60 percent of his or her time there.

Mechanical skills—valuable if the leader must solve mechanical problems. For example, the manager of an auto repair shop must assist the trained mechanics in diagnosing transmission problems.

Organizational skills—important if the leader must coordinate activities, schedule and plan events, or organize work.

Skills training—most skills training can be done quickly and locally. If it cannot, the leader must have the skills prior to selection. For example, if a leader lacks speaking skills necessary for the job, classes can be taken. If the leader needs training on nuclear waste disposal, there is a good chance that the training will not be widely and easily available.

Writing skills—this is important if the leader will be communicating regularly by memos, reports, working papers, briefs, or letters with constituents. In some cases, administrative assistants may write or at least edit documents, but that is not true in all situations. Twenty years ago, all leaders had secretaries. Now, with the widespread use of word processing and downsizing, this is rare.

Management or Leadership Experience

Assistant manager experience—an opportunity to practice completing some of the tasks of a manager is appropriate for moving up into a management position in a large restaurant, for example.

Leadership experience—chairing a committee is valuable experience before being elected to the presidency of a social club. Leadership of community groups is valuable experience for a prospective leader of a community or government agency, or an executive of a company.

Management experience—this would be important before moving into an executive position. The level of management experience necessary would vary by the size and type of organization. An individual should have at least vice president experience with a comparable organization before becoming the CEO of a Fortune 500 company.

Management trainee—training is valuable before starting an entry-level management position. For example, if someone works as a management trainee for three years, he or she may be ready for a first-line supervisor or assistant manager position.

Vice president of the United States, governor, or senator—such experience would qualify someone to be president.

Work experience, but no management experience—appropriate for first-line supervisory positions.

Special Abilities, Traits, and Characteristics

Ability to deal with frustration and ambiguity—this will be helpful in difficult situations.

Appearing to be self-confident—this is important in most leadership positions since making followers feel that the leader knows the score is one of the most important jobs of a leader. In some cases, it may be the only role that a leader must play.

Attitudes toward others—as they relate to the organization. In other words, people who dislike teenagers should not work in administrative positions in high schools. People with strong prejudices toward minorities should not work in leadership positions in law enforcement.

Cleanliness—critical in health care and sales situations.

Considerate—in most organizations, showing consideration to followers and constituents is critical.

Consistent values—every organization has core values that drive behavior. Every candidate should share those basic organizational values.

Creativity—this trait is particularly useful when finding new approaches to problems, when leading a creative team, and when heading an R & D group.

Education—set this standard as low as you can while still getting the work done effectively. The higher the level of education required, the more expensive the position and the harder it is to fill the spot. For example, do you really need a PhD to be an effective vice president of executive development? On the other hand, the dean of the business school at a major university must have one. Do not use the incumbent in the position to determine the level of education necessary. CEOs used to move up the ranks from the mail room, often without any college degree. That rarely works anymore.

Family oriented—required if the organization advocates a balance between work and personal life. Note that this does not mean that the leader has to have a family, but rather that he or she must value the philosophy.

Future oriented—important if the organization requires extensive change.

Health and fitness—extremely important if the leader must be counted on regularly and cannot be easily replaced. A certain level of health and fitness is critical if a leader has a stressful and demanding job and if you are hiring for the long term. This includes both physical and mental health.

Initiative—this is important if the leader can set his or her own work agenda. In a highly structured environment, lower or midlevel leaders do not always need initiative.

Intelligence—it would be hard to think of a situation where a group would not be better off with an intelligent leader. However, the level of intelligence may not have to be superior in all organizations.

Interpersonal skills—it is critical that a leader be able to effectively interact with others. There is no such thing as a leader without followers.

Participative versus authoritarian style of leadership—a participative style is valuable in social clubs and organizations where there is a high level of expertise among followers. For example, in your ski club, an authoritarian would be an inappropriate president.

Past oriented—valuable for leaders of stable organizations with strong cultures and traditions that must be maintained or organizations that must do extensive problem solving.

Persistence—in most high-level endeavors, including leadership, persistence is a valuable trait. It would be most important when tasks take a long time, when achievement is not quickly earned, or when working through other people.

Present oriented—important for operational leaders.

Visionary—most leadership positions do not require a visionary leader, but some do.

Scenarios of Organizations That Need Leaders

The scenarios follow. Fill in the blanks.

SCENARIO 1: PRESIDENT OF SUNSHINE FISHING CLUB

Imagine that you are a member of a small fishing club in the southeastern United States. This is primarily a social organization that takes three major fishing trips per year around the United States. The current president is leaving for health reasons. He has been leading the club for ten years and has arranged many great trips. The president leads meetings, researches various sites, handles all finances, contacts members to gather information, maintains the membership roster, orients new members, and keeps archival records of all previous trips, including photographs. In exchange, the president's trips are paid for by the membership. The members are in agreement that they would like to maintain the current leader's list of tasks and choose someone who can maintain their traditions. List the attributes necessary for the new leader.

Desired outcomes and objectives: _____

_____

_____

_____

_____

Personality: _____

_____

_____
_____
_____

Technical skills: _____
_____
_____
_____
_____

Management/leadership experience: _____
_____
_____
_____
_____

Special abilities/traits/characteristics: _____
_____
_____
_____
_____

Scenario 2: Vice President of Planning for a Fortune 500 Company

Assume that you are the vice president of human resources for a large corporation headquartered in Chicago. You have been assigned to recruit candidates for vice president of planning for the company. This is a new position and a new department created by the president. The vice president of planning will be in charge of all strategic planning for the entire corporation. The work will be done department by department, division by division. At the end of the process, an overall plan will be developed and introduced to the entire management team. The strategic plan will be reviewed and updated at every level biannually. It is anticipated that a staff of approximately five professional and two administrative workers will be necessary to complete the work of the planning department. The company has been seeing a decline in market share recently and has had cost increases. Planning has always been haphazard in the past.

Desired outcomes and objectives: _____

_____

_____

_____

_____

Personality: _____

_____

_____

_____

_____

Technical skills: _____

_____

_____

_____

_____

Management/leadership experience: _____

_____

_____

_____

_____

Special abilities/traits/characteristics: _____

_____

_____

_____

_____

SCENARIO 3: HIGH SCHOOL PRINCIPAL

A southwestern high school needs a new principal. The current principal has taken a job with another district and will leave in June. The high school has 1,200 students ranging from ninth to twelfth grade. It is located in rural Texas and spreads out across the county. The student population is diverse, equally represented by white, Mexican American, and Native American students with a smaller number of transient African American students whose parents are stationed at a nearby military base. The socio-economic status is primarily middle class, with a few outliers on both ends of the spectrum, and most children live on farms and ranches. Both academics and athletics are important to the residents of this district. High school sports are the main entertainment for the residents of the county. About half of the students will go to college. The school board and the parents are advocates of strong discipline, and few major problems occur. Funding schools is always an issue in the district. Minor race issues have occurred recently.

Desired outcomes and objectives: _____

_____

_____

_____

_____

Personality: _____

_____

_____

_____

_____

Technical skills: _____

_____

_____

_____

_____

Management/leadership experience: _____

_____

_____

_____

_____

Special abilities/traits/characteristics: _____

_____

_____

_____

_____

SCENARIO 4: DIRECTOR OF PUBLIC RELATIONS
FOR A HISTORICAL SOCIETY

The board of a state-supported historical society in the Northwest is seeking a new director of public relations. Given recent drastic declines in revenue in the state, many citizens and politicians want to cut so-called expendable agencies and departments. Despite the threats to its budget, the historical society board and the governor consider the preservation of the state's historical sites to be of the utmost importance. Besides their historical significance, these sites bring in tourism dollars. The director of public relations must interact with the public and with state and local legislators and office holders, seek federal grants for programming, plan and supervise the promotion of the historical sites, and respond to all media inquiries.

Desired outcomes and objectives: _____

_____

_____

_____

_____

Personality: _____

_____

_____

_____

_____

Technical skills: _____

_____

_____

_____

_____

Management/leadership experience: _____

_____

_____

_____

_____

Special abilities/traits/characteristics: _____

_____

_____

_____

_____

SCENARIO 5: MAYOR OF A MIDSIZED CITY IN THE RUST BELT

Both political parties of this city are struggling to come up with viable candidates for the mayoral race in the fall. The city has lost half of its manufacturing jobs over the past fifteen years. The population is aging because the number of young people leaving the area after high school and college is increasing. They cannot find jobs. The weather is bad six months of the year. The politics are old school—some city council members are in their seventies. The city has been run the same way that it was when there were lots of jobs and lots of revenue. Interest in running for a government office has been on the decline. Political appointees staff most of the city offices. Finding funding for a candidate is not the issue. The issue is finding the right kind of individual who is willing and talented enough to seek and implement solutions to the city's problems.

Desired outcomes and objectives: _____

_____

_____

_____

_____

Personality: _____

_____

_____

_____

_____

Technical skills: _____

_____

_____

_____

_____

Management/leadership experience: _____

_____

_____

_____

_____

Special abilities/traits/characteristics: _____

_____

_____

_____

_____

SCENARIO 6: CEO OF A LARGE URBAN HOSPITAL

The CEO of a large hospital in Seattle is retiring. This hospital is operating in the black, although only about three-quarters of the 1,500 beds are full at any point in time. There has been a recent shift toward shorter stays for patients, and outpatient surgery is being performed at the hospital's surgery centers in the suburbs. The new CEO has to find ways to use the beds more efficiently and to move some operations to suburban areas. The outgoing CEO has been quite successful and is well respected in the community. She is willing to help with the selection process and is more aware than anyone that the current style of serving patients must change if the hospital is going to survive. The hospital board is strong and supportive. The hospital is well equipped and staffed and the facilities are state-of-the-art.

Desired outcomes and objectives: _____

_____

_____

_____

_____

Personality: _____

_____

_____

_____

_____

Technical skills: _____

_____

_____

_____

_____

Management/leadership experience: _____

_____

_____

_____

_____

Special abilities/traits/characteristics: _____

_____

_____

_____

Complete the exercise before reading further.

Sample Attribute Choices

The following are my lists for each scenario. Please note that there are no right answers that can be set in stone, but there are answers that make sense given the descriptions of the scenarios.

SCENARIO 1: PRESIDENT OF SUNSHINE FISHING CLUB

Desired outcomes and objectives: The president of the club must call and organize all meetings. The leader must honestly manage the finances of the club, which includes substantial fees paid by the members for the trips. The leader must successfully research and plan three week-long fishing trips per year.

Personality: Honest, conscientious, optimistic, friendly, an interest in other people, emotionally stable, likes fishing.

Technical skills: Good fishing skills, planning and organizing skills, should handle large sums of money well, must possess an understanding of or willingness to learn the travel business.

Management/leadership experience: Minimal leadership experience necessary, but it would be helpful if the leader had worked with the outgoing president on previous trips and tasks.

Special abilities/traits/characteristics: Values the traditions of the club, present oriented with a strong interest in the past. Flexible schedule that allows the leader time to plan the trips, conduct meetings, and handle the work of the organization. Must show initiative. Must be healthy and fit. Creative. Smart.

SCENARIO 2: VICE PRESIDENT OF PLANNING FOR A FORTUNE 500 COMPANY

Desired outcomes and objectives: The vice president will develop and communicate a complex strategic plan for every department in every division in the organization. Progress toward achieving the plan must be measured continuously and the plan must be updated annually.

Personality: Conscientious, cooperative, optimistic, high energy level.

Technical skills: Very strong computer skills, organizational skills, excellent writing skills, broad business knowledge, knowledge of the industry and the law.

Management/leadership experience: Should have management experience in a similar environment. It need not be executive experience, but the candidates should have interacted with executives in their previous job.

Special abilities/traits/characteristics: Future oriented, consistent values, positive attitude toward all aspects of business. Must show initiative. MBA required. Should use a participative style of leadership. Must be self-confident and persistent. Should have specific experience with strategic planning as well as extensive training in this area. Very intelligent.

SCENARIO 3: HIGH SCHOOL PRINCIPAL

Desired outcomes and objectives: Maintain the traditions of the school and the community. Ensure good discipline in the school. Keep the number of problems in the school down. Continue to monitor both the academic and sports programs with the goal of maintaining high standards for both.

Personality: Conscientious, extroverted, optimistic, salty, honest, high energy level, calm, emotionally stable.

Technical skills: Must be state certified to be a school administrator and teacher. Must have strong knowledge of education, teaching, and administration.

Management/leadership experience: Should have served as a principal of a smaller school or as an assistant principal of a school of comparable size. Must have been a leader of some community organization.

Special abilities/traits/characteristics: Present oriented with a strong interest in past traditions. Family oriented. Consistent values. Positive attitude toward children. Must be detail oriented and willing to constantly monitor performance data. Must have an undergraduate degree in education and a master's degree in educational administration. Considerate toward teachers and staff. Strong interpersonal skills. Persistent and self-confident.

SCENARIO 4: DIRECTOR OF PUBLIC RELATIONS FOR A HISTORICAL SOCIETY

Desired outcomes and objectives: Must constantly present the society in a positive light. All potential public relations problems must be handled immediately and must leave a positive impression with the public and the state legislators. Must respond quickly to all requests for information. Organize promotion and increase attendance at historical sites.

Personality: Conscientious, extroverted, friendly, cooperative, optimistic, high energy level.

Technical skills: Excellent writing skills, knowledge of the media and public relations, basic knowledge of and willingness to learn about the historical society, influence skills, strong knowledge of marketing, advertising, and promotion.

Management/leadership experience: Previous management experience in public relations.

Special abilities/traits/characteristics: Future oriented. Consistent values. Strong positive attitude about the value of the work of the society. Ability to deal with frustration and ambiguity. Self-confident, very strong interpersonal skills, smart, creative.

SCENARIO 5: MAYOR OF A MIDSIZED CITY IN THE RUST BELT

Desired outcomes and objectives: Must attract industry to city. Must find ways to make city more attractive by initiating winter events that will get regional attention. Must find ways to keep young citizens from leaving. Must break through traditional approaches to government.

Personality: Conscientious, extroverted, friendly, cooperative, optimistic, authentic, honest, high energy level, emotionally stable.

Technical skills: Strong organizational skills, understanding of or willingness to learn about local laws and government at all levels, very strong speaking skills, very strong influence skills.

Management/leadership experience: Five to ten years of leadership experience in both professional and community organizations.

Special abilities/traits/characteristics: Highly future oriented. Must show initiative. Very intelligent. Must possess a college degree. Healthy and fit, visionary, considerate, strong interpersonal skills, persistent, able to deal with frustration and ambiguity. Creative, self-confident, willing to travel and meet with corporate decision makers.

Scenario 6: CEO of a Large Urban Hospital

Desired outcomes and objectives: Must develop new service delivery options. Must maintain the hospital's reputation. Must maintain current staffing, equipment, and facility levels. Must follow in the steps of a highly respected CEO. Must find ways to cut costs without hurting patient care.

Personality: Conscientious, extroverted, friendly, cooperative, optimistic, honest, high energy level, calm, emotionally stable.

Technical skills: Organizational skills, strong understanding of hospital administration and health care, knowledge of health care law, influence skills.

Management/leadership experience: Must have previous executive (vice president level) experience in health care.

Special abilities/traits/characteristics: Future oriented with strong respect for tradition. Consistent values. Positive attitude toward patients and health care professionals. Must show initiative. Clean, healthy, and fit. Visionary, considerate, highly intelligent, strong interpersonal skills, persistent, self-confident, creative. Must possess master's degree in health care administration or comparable field.

Write Your Own Scenario

Now, think about a leadership position important to you. You create scenario 7. What organization or group, of which you are currently a member, is in need of a leader? Maybe it is a social group. Maybe it is your company. Maybe it is the national government. Name and describe the leader, the level in the organization, and the situation. Then complete the same exercise by listing the attributes in the blanks.

Scenario 7: _____

_____

_____

_____

_____

_____

_____

_____

_____

_____

_____

_____

Desired outcomes and objectives: _____

_____

_____

_____

_____

Personality: _____

_____

_____

_____

_____

Technical skills: _____

_____

_____

_____

Management/leadership experience: _____

_____

_____

_____

_____

Special abilities/traits/characteristics: _____

_____

_____

_____

Now that we have identified the attributes necessary for leaders in specific situations, we must find candidates for the positions and pick just the right people. The next five chapters explain the recruiting and selection of leaders. Chapter 4 focuses specifically on recruiting.

4

Recruiting Leaders

How does your organization recruit candidates for leadership positions? Two approaches to recruiting are commonly used. The first is reactive—advertising an opening for a position and hoping a good candidate applies for the job. This strategy is the one most commonly used by most groups, whether they are social clubs or Fortune 500 companies. The second approach is proactive—aggressively seeking candidates for openings based on specific criteria.

When it comes to filling leadership positions, there are two other approaches. The third approach is the power play. This means that a leader or would-be leader sees a power gap and uses a variety of strategies to secure the position. A fourth approach is to simply let the cream rise to the top. Some organizations move managers up in lockstep regardless of changing needs and changing people. Depending on the type of position and the organization, any of these approaches might produce a qualified candidate for the job.

Unfortunately, the cream is not always what rises. Therefore, as recruiters we need to do a better job. How do I know this? Look around you. Putting corporate, government, and religious scandals aside (if you can), there is a leadership gap in our organizations. This is common knowledge, but if you are unsure, take some time to read what the leadership experts are saying. During interviews, I have been shocked to find how poorly qualified some candidates for leadership positions in my organization have been. This was particularly bad news since we spent many hours and days seeking and screening and we thought that we had invited only the best to interview. My colleagues in business, government, and community agencies tell similar stories.

Obviously, a proactive approach is best. However, it is not without its pitfalls. A proactive approach is time consuming. Followers, human resource professionals, and hiring superiors must spend hours developing and executing a recruiting strategy. It is so much easier to run an ad and pray. A second problem is that some people may get their feelings hurt if they feel entitled to a promotion. This belief may be based on tradition, past practices, long tenure, having performed many tedious and difficult tasks, promises made by managers, pressure from family members, and other events. It is hard to pass over hopeful members of an organization to hire an outsider or an outlier. Thus we often hire the one in line for the promotion to spare ourselves the grief and the impact on morale.

Many times, we let the choice of a leader go because we do not want to make the decision. There are all kinds of reasons why we may not want to make a leadership decision. If we choose not to decide, then we can think it is not our fault when things go wrong. We may not decide because we feel hopeless. We may not think that we have any stake in choosing the leader. Sometimes, we are lazy. Often we do not know what to look for or how to decide. This book is designed to address that reason.

Several steps are necessary to execute an effective recruiting strategy. First, you must carefully identify what you are looking for. You did that in chapter 3. Second, you must think about where people with the attributes or qualifications you listed might be living and working. Third, you need to contact candidates and screen them for the basic attributes important to the position. Finally, you must sell your organization and clarify its objectives for the candidates. You must convince qualified individuals to apply for the position. Recruiting is done when you have created a pool of qualified candidates. That means that you have a group (usually three to ten people, depending on the level of the position and the size of the organization) of individuals who appear to have all of the basic attributes that you are seeking, are interested in the leadership position, would accept the job if it was offered to them, and are willing to go through the selection process. Let's take it one step at a time.

Step 1: Carefully Identify What You Are Looking For

We did that in chapter 3. Move on to step 2.

Step 2: Locate Potential Candidates

Finding potential candidates requires knowledge of other organizations that do similar things. For example, if nominating a candidate for president of the United States, you need to identify leaders at other levels of government who have similar expertise, including governors, senators, and others with large-scale government experience. This search must be done at the broad national level, but not globally since the president must be born in the United States. If you are hiring a general manager who will be groomed to become the CEO of your plastics company, you need to identify successful managers in other plastics firms. The search may be done regionally if there is an adequate number of similar companies in the area or nationally if not. You may even need to look internationally if the company does business overseas.

The key is to list the organizations where people with the expertise you are seeking might be currently working. If there are many in your area, you may be able to find good candidates locally. If not, you will have to broaden the search. The best way to approach this task is to work through professional associations, at both regional and national levels. Often, these associations have annual national meetings where you can meet with others in the field. The networking that you do at such meetings can provide good opportunities to discuss current industry issues, listen to possible candidates make presentations, and interact informally with others who have similar interests and experience. Frequently, these associations, whether work related or social organizations, have newsletters or journals where you could strategically place well-written ads or articles for people who have the expertise you desire.

If you are filling a leadership role in a social or interest club, the best source will likely be local members. Which members have taken on special projects? Which members attend most meetings? Which members have given the most time to the group? Sometimes people will volunteer to run for office in a club in order to pad their resume. You are most interested in finding the members who are actually involved in the regular activities of the club. The outgoing president may know the most about who has contributed to the group.

Some have qualms about recruiting from other organizations. For example, they wonder if it is fair to recruit a very good assistant principal away from a neighboring school. It is your responsibility to find and recruit the best-qualified person for the job. If there is a moral dilemma about leaving a particular organization, that is up to the candidate to decide. Loyalty to one's employer is admirable, but people must do what is best for their own careers and families if opportunities do not exist in their organizations. However, if you learn that a candidate reneged on a deal to stay with an employer after receiving tuition reimbursement for an MBA, it will tell you something about what you might expect.

There may be certain parts of the country where you will need to focus your recruiting. For example, Hartford, Connecticut is a center for the insurance industry. Instead of placing ads in the classified section of your local newspaper when searching for the vice president of underwriting, you may want to run ads in the business section of the Hartford newspaper or papers in other cities like Columbus, Ohio, and New York where large insurance companies are found. If the job was in automobile parts, Detroit might be the right place to run an ad. You should know where to find your counterparts and your competitors. They are the most likely source of potential candidates for leadership positions.

Whenever possible, attend meetings and conferences where qualified candidates might be exhibiting their talents. For example, if you are recruiting a general manager for a manufacturing plant, attend a conference in your field. Make it a point to attend sessions conducted by practicing managers. Pay attention to the programs they describe, the initiatives they have implemented, the goals that they have set for their organizations, and the way they communicate. You may be able to recruit them during the conference. You can obtain their business cards or papers they distribute. Make notes and contact them later. You can get a good work sample without them even knowing that you are watching. Do the same with journals in your field. Often, practitioners write articles about new projects and ideas that they have tried. When you find ideas consistent with your organization's culture and goals, contact the authors and talk about their careers and your job.

Let's go back to our examples and practice identifying potential candidates and where they might be found one at a time.

Scenario 1: President of Sunshine Fishing Club

This will be an internal search among the membership of the club. Only if there is a shortage of members would you need to go outside. If that is the case, a membership drive should precede the search for a president.

Scenario 2: Vice President of Planning for a Fortune 500 Company

If the company is located in a major U.S. city or near one or more high-quality MBA programs, this search may be local. In most cases, you will need to search at least regionally. It would be a good idea to advertise in an industry journal, do personal recruiting at industry trade shows and conferences (note the people making presentations on planning), and talk with colleagues in other companies. Perhaps one of your suppliers or customers has a person who has been doing planning and who is ready for a promotion that is not available at that company. Another source might be a midlevel manager or director in your company or another organization who earned an MBA and has taken one or more good strategic planning courses. You might also want to consider individuals who have performed well in another function, have done planning for community associations or clubs, and are willing to complete courses to learn to develop and execute a strategic plan.

Scenario 3: High School Principal

The first thing to find are the districts in your region that have similar values and priorities. Then contact the assistant principals in your district and comparable districts. Unless this is an unusual location, you should be able to fill this position within the county, or within the area of a few counties in the worst-case scenario. In addition, there are numerous meetings of school administrators. Talk to local superintendents about people they might know who are ready for a promotion. Circulate at conferences and meetings and let assistant principals know that you have a job that you need to fill. Teachers in the area would also be a good source of information about good assistant principals. Review area newspapers for articles about good things going on in other districts. Note the names of the individuals coordinating these projects. As an ongoing task, make a note of interesting, talented people whenever you meet them. You never know when you may have an opening.

SCENARIO 4: DIRECTOR OF PUBLIC RELATIONS FOR A HISTORICAL SOCIETY

It is easier to scout for talent for this position than any others listed. The reason is because a group with excellent public relations is highly visible—that is what you are seeking too! Read the paper and industry journals. Watch the news. Talk to citizens in the city or county where you live. Which community groups, businesses, and government agencies have the best reputations, make the papers frequently, handle problems quickly, appear to wear Teflon (bad news never sticks), and tend to run the most effective ads? Narrow the search down to the groups that are most similar to yours. Find the people who are in charge of public relations in those organizations and ask if they are interested. If they are not, they may have a staff member who has been learning from them. Contact area colleges to see if they have an alumnus who has done well and might be interested in returning to the area.

SCENARIO 5: MAYOR OF A MIDSIZED CITY IN THE RUST BELT

Obviously, you will look first at local political supporters. Who has been involved in campaigns, speaks up at meetings, volunteers for special projects? Who has strong speaking skills and is committed to the area? Next, look at community leaders outside of political campaigns and government. Which of these individuals exhibits the attributes you are seeking? Although we tend to think that lawyers, doctors, educators, and business managers are not willing to leave their "lucrative" jobs for politics, many do. In fact, the ones who are best off financially may be the ones most willing to try something new and enjoy the challenge. In addition, they often feel that they owe the community for their success.

SCENARIO 6: CEO OF A LARGE URBAN HOSPITAL

This will be a national search. You will be looking at vice presidents of large urban hospitals and CEOs of smaller hospitals all over the country. The best way to identify them will be through professional and industry associations. Place notices in their journals, attend conferences, network at professional meetings, and go to presentations made by working hospital executives. You may also want to consider using a search firm for a position like this. They will have databases of potential candidates who want to do a search in a confidential manner. Do your homework before contacting search firms and then interview them to make sure you choose the right one with which to work. The fees are often very high, but a national search is difficult and expensive in any case.

Step 3: Contact and Screen Potential Candidates

Identify which of the attributes that you listed in the previous chapter are tangible skills. These are the attributes that are inflexible, in terms of the search requirements. Note that intangible qualities like honesty, organizational skills, and initiative will be tested later in the selection process using other techniques. By tangible attributes, I mean things like the following:

- Years of experience
- College degree(s) and majors
- Types of organizations where candidates have worked
- Certifications, licensures, professional designations (e.g., CPA or CLU)
- Types and levels of positions held

Once you have found five to fifteen likely candidates (the number you need will depend on the level of the position—the higher the level, the fewer qualified candidates you will find), schedule informal meetings or telephone conversations with each one. I would call it a meeting at this time rather than an interview and schedule an hour with each individual. If you are recruiting aggressively, many of these potential candidates may not have formally applied for the position yet.

Begin this meeting with an explanation of why you contacted this person, and why you think he or she may be qualified and may be someone you might want to hire. Establish the fact that the individual would be willing to consider another position if the opportunity is right. If you are recruiting someone who is not willing to relocate, for personal reasons or because of a commitment to the current employer, it is pointless to pursue this candidate.

If you have an application or a resume, you can ask specific questions about the person's experience. Whether you have an application or not, stick with the basics in your questions. Ask about each of the required tangible attributes using closed-ended questions. For example, what college degrees do you hold? What was your major? Where did you work previously? How long were you there? Do you have an administrative certificate? Have you completed the appropriate training? Did you take a course on strategic planning? At this point, you are trying to determine if the individual has the basic requirements for the job. During this meeting, move on to step 4 if the individual has the basic qualifications you are seeking. If not, tell him or her politely that you must find a candidate who is a CPA or who has an MBA. If this has been a pleasant experience, the individual may even help you recruit someone who is better qualified. Let's practice this for each of our scenarios:

Tangible Attributes and Position Requirements for Each Scenario

SCENARIO 1: PRESIDENT OF SUNSHINE FISHING CLUB

Membership in the club

At least ten years fishing experience

Experience handling money for an organization

Experience traveling and fishing in various locations

Basic understanding of or willingness to learn the travel business

Flexible schedule

Healthy and fit

SCENARIO 2: VICE PRESIDENT OF PLANNING FOR A FORTUNE 500 COMPANY

Very strong computer skills

Excellent writing skills

Knowledge of the industry and the law

Management experience in a similar environment

MBA

Specific strategic planning experience and training

SCENARIO 3: HIGH SCHOOL PRINCIPAL

Must be state certified to be a school administrator and teacher

Strong knowledge of education, teaching, and administration

Teaching experience

Experience as a principal of a smaller school or as an assistant principal of a school of comparable size

Experience as a leader of some community organization

Undergraduate degree in education

Master's degree in educational administration

SCENARIO 4: DIRECTOR OF PUBLIC RELATIONS
FOR A HISTORICAL SOCIETY

Excellent writing skills

Knowledge of the media and public relations

Basic knowledge of and willingness to learn about the historical society

Strong knowledge of marketing, advertising, and promotion

Previous management experience in public relations

Degree in communications with coursework in public relations

SCENARIO 5: MAYOR OF A MIDSIZED CITY IN THE RUST BELT

Understanding of or willingness to learn about local laws and government at all levels

Very strong speaking skills

Five to ten years of leadership experience in both professional and community organizations

A college degree

Healthy and fit

Willingness to travel and meet with corporate decision makers

SCENARIO 6: CEO OF A LARGE URBAN HOSPITAL

Strong understanding of hospital administration and health care

Knowledge of the law in the field

Must have previous executive (vice president level) experience in health care

Master's degree in health care administration or comparable field

SCENARIO 7: YOUR POSITION

_____

_____

_____

_____

_____

_____

Step 4: Sell the Leadership Position

You must convince qualified individuals to apply for the leadership position. This entails selling not just the job, the organization, and yourself, but also the job location. When recruiting leaders, senior-level experienced professionals should be doing the recruiting, not the same human resources staff recruiter who visits colleges. This professional may be the director of human resources, the CEO, the vice president of the area where the job is located, or even a board member—this depends on the position. Using a professional soft-selling approach, talk about the leadership position and its importance to the organization. Bring along marketing materials designed to sell your products and services and your organization. You may also want to include news stories about the organization, press releases, and internal publications. These materials should be limited to the ones that best present the organization and do not overwhelm a prospective candidate. They

should be materials that demonstrate the culture and values of the organization. Talk about why you work in this organization and what it has done
for you professionally and personally.

What do you do if the position is not attractive? What if the location is
lousy, the pay is terrible, the job is thankless, the leader will be abused by
all the constituents, and the work is not satisfying? Change it. If you
cannot, you should leave the organization. No, I am not joking.

Internal Recruiting

If an organization is large enough and uses an internal labor market
(i.e., the strategy is to hire only at the entry level and promote from
within), recruiting will be done inside. This approach has advantages and
disadvantages. Let's review both.

Advantages of Internal Recruiting

1. The candidates know the organization and may be familiar with
   the work done in the position—the positive and negative aspects.
2. The organization has a track record with the candidates for the
   leadership position—past performance is a predictor of future performance.
3. Internal recruiting is easy, quick, and cheap.
4. Promoting from within is a good motivational tool.
5. Internal candidates are used to doing things the organization's way.

Disadvantages of Internal Recruiting

1. Employees in organizations with internal labor market strategies
   look at promotions as entitlements, whether they have the necessary skills or not.
2. The number of candidates is limited to the number of employees
   who have the necessary qualifications and experience.
3. If the internal candidate is not selected and an external candidate
   is, there could be negative motivational repercussions.

4. If one internal candidate is selected over another internal candidate, there could be negative motivational repercussions.
5. Internal candidates are used to doing things the organization's way.

If you get the impression that I am opposed to internal candidates for leadership positions, you would be both right and wrong. For first-line supervisory positions and midlevel management positions, it is a very good idea to promote from within if the organization does not require new and innovative approaches. For high-level leadership positions, both internal and external candidates should be found and considered.

One mistake that is frequently made with internal candidates is that they are not put through the same screening procedure, out of either carelessness or embarrassment. We may be careless or lazy and not want to bother testing internal candidates because we assume that we know them. We may also be embarrassed to ask an experienced manager to go through the same process as an outside candidate. That is a big mistake. Internal candidates must be screened using the identical selection tools that are used for external candidates. If the attributes that have been identified as essential to the position are important, every candidate must be screened in the same manner. If the attributes are not really important, get rid of them for all candidates.

When you have at least three to ten prescreened qualified and interested individuals, you will begin the selection process. The actual number needed will depend on the organization, the level of the position, location, pay, and required attributes. Jobs that require a PhD will have fewer applicants because few people have a doctorate. Positions in small social clubs like the fishing club will have few available candidates because the search is limited to members. However, there should be at least four qualified candidates for director of public relations since there are many qualified people from all over the country.

Effective recruiting is an investment of time and money. You can cross your fingers and hope that good candidates apply or you can aggressively seek the best-qualified people for the position. Either way, you will pay. The way that you approach this process will determine the quality of leader you select. Chapter 5 will help you find the right selection tools.

Leadership Selection Tools

A variety of tools may be used to select the right person for a leadership position. Sometimes, organizations use the cloudy mirror test—if the individual clouds up a mirror when breathing on it, he or she gets the job. This occurs most often when no one wants the presidency of the club or to be the church deacon—few people have the drive and energy for leadership when it does not pay. It also occurs when promotions are given—the person with the most seniority gets the job. However, for promotional opportunities, the people making the decision must use more comprehensive strategies to pick the right person.

The selection tool used most often in business is the unstructured interview, which has about as much validity as the cloudy mirror test. In chapter 7, I explain selection interviews and teach readers how to develop and use valid and reliable structured interviews. In addition, there are other good tools that should be used along with a structured interview to assist you in selecting the right person.

Verify the Tangible Required Attributes and Qualifications

To begin, verify the tangible attributes and qualifications identified in chapter 4. You should do this only with the finalists that you have chosen to put through the selection process. You may be asking, "Who would lie about a college degree or work experience?" You will be amazed at how many people do both. If the qualification is required to perform the job well, check to make sure the candidate has it.

Call the human resources departments of former employers to verify that candidates held the positions they claimed. Most employers will confirm past employment and dates of employment. You can ask why the individual left the company, but many organizations will not provide that information. I strongly recommend that you do not try to gather confidential information from individuals who do employment verifications. Typically, they do not know any more than the records indicate and most will not provide additional information due to corporate policy.

Do not call a candidate's current employers, because you could jeopardize their employment. However, you may want to visit the organization's Web site to verify the candidate's title and contact information. You could also read company reports or news stories which would verify that candidates have the position they claim.

College degrees can be verified by calling the registrar's office of the college or university that the individual claims to have attended. This should be done whenever a college degree is necessary for a position. The date of graduation may be required to verify that the individual earned a degree. Be sure to ask specifically about the degree earned. Many people attend a college briefly and then indicate dates of attendance on their resume, suggesting that a degree was earned when it was not. If candidates must have a degree in a professional field, you may want to require that official transcripts be sent from the colleges directly to you. Note that an official transcript will come directly from the college and will contain the raised seal of the institution.

Professional designations can be verified by contacting the professional association or accrediting or licensing board. If they cannot provide the information, you should be suspicious and ask the candidate for an official transcript or other documentation of the designation. Government licenses or certifications can be documented through government offices. In the film *Catch Me if You Can*, the main character poses as a professional in fields requiring very specific training. Although most people would not try to pass themselves off as a lawyer, a doctor, or an airplane pilot, many people do exaggerate their credentials. For example, it is not difficult for an accountant to pose as a CPA.

For most senior-level leadership positions, you should perform a criminal background check and a credit check. There are many companies that will provide this service for a nominal fee. If the possibilities of conflict of interest, fraud, or corruption exist on this job, both credit and criminal background checks should be done on the candidates. (All candidates should be informed prior to performing such checks.) If you have a small candidate pool, you may want to do this before you use the other selection tools. All of the selection tools that I discuss take time and many cost money, so you may as well start with a base of candidates who are employable.

Develop a Selection Strategy

Developing a selection strategy requires that you review the rest of the attributes and decide which selection tool will best assess the candidates' ability to do the job. I recommend that several tools be utilized for each position. I include the selection tools that will provide the most benefit for choosing organizational leaders. For detailed information about all selection tools available to decision makers, see Heneman and Judge's *Staffing Organizations.*[1] Here are some tools that you will find useful as well as an explanation of each.

1. *A structured interview.* The next chapter provides a complete explanation of this tool. Research supports the use of structured interviews even when good cognitive ability tests are also used. This approach can be used effectively across jobs.

2. *Cognitive ability testing.* These tests can determine general ability (basic intelligence—a good predictor of performance across jobs), mechanical ability, verbal ability, mathematical ability, and so on. Many large organizations have professionals in their human resources departments who are qualified to use a variety of tests. If not, a good testing service can help identify appropriate tests that effectively measure the desired attributes. To arrange for testing, contact your human resources department. They should be able to arrange for the testing by a reputable firm.

Research tells us that this testing is the most effective type of selection tool because it predicts technical skills, but it is not necessary for most leadership positions. A mechanical ability test (one type of cognitive ability test) would be very useful when hiring someone at the entry level for a maintenance job. However, the manager of an automobile dealership's service center, for example, has probably proven his mechanical ability through his work over a period of years. You could review performance and training evaluations instead of testing in a situation like this.

For most leadership positions, a measure of general ability would be helpful. Basic intelligence is considered a general ability and is a good predictor of performance across jobs. Note, however, that very high intelligence is not necessarily a quality needed for all leadership positions. In addition, if the leader is responsible for oral or written presentations, a verbal ability test would be helpful if samples of previous presentations or writing are not available.

3. *Personality testing.* Personality tests can help you identify which candidates can work well as part of a team, interact effectively with others, and handle stress well. Personality tests tell us about conscientiousness, emotional stability, extroversion, openness to change, and many other traits that might be necessary to successfully perform in a leadership position. Many of us consider ourselves to be good judges of character, but it can be difficult to determine personality by meeting someone in an artificial situation like an interview. If we meet a candidate in a social situation, we may confuse gregariousness with being under the influence. Again, a testing service can provide valid and reliable tests for use in your selection process. Use experts for all of your testing needs.

4. *Honesty testing.* Paper-and-pencil tests can help you identify the candidates who are most likely to steal or commit fraud. There are some ethical concerns about the use of these questionnaires, but most large retailers have been using them for years with success. Lie detector tests cannot be used for selection. If you are filling a job where the employee would have access to valuable information or supplies, an honesty test could be very helpful. Again, work with an expert to find the right test.

5. *Work samples and performance tests.* Look at samples of the candidates' previous work. If you are hiring a marketing or public relations director, ask for a portfolio of promotional materials candidates developed in previous jobs. The samples of work that you request should reflect the type of situations that are actually encountered in your organization and in the specific leadership role. You must outline the "right answers" before using tests. For example, what types of audiovisuals do you want leaders in your organization to use when making a presentation? PowerPoint slides? Observe each candidate making a short speech to see if you are getting the right answer. Evaluate each candidate using the same standard. This is a highly effective selection tool if designed correctly.

6. *Job applications.* Please note that some organizations use a common application for all jobs. If that is not required, create your own application

form for the position. This way, it can be tailored to the opening. You want to gather only specific information about a leader candidate's education and experience relevant to your selection qualifications. This is your best opportunity to have candidates list each previously held position with dates of employment, dates and places that college degrees were earned, and lists of professional credentials. You can use the application to verify information. Additionally, if a candidate has lied about a qualification, you have it in writing. This also eliminates potential confusion when a candidate verbally details his or her qualifications. Be sure that every question is job related. In other words, do not ask about military experience unless that is a job requirement. The application should contain a place for candidates to signify that the information they provide is accurate. Some organizations may assign weights to specific items and create a numerical score for each candidate based on the application.

7. *References.* Valuable references should come from people who observed the candidate's work. These people can provide answers to specific questions regarding technical and professional expertise. Evaluate the objectiveness and competence of the referee when determining the usefulness of the reference. In general, personal references are absolutely terrible sources of information about performance skills—they are not reliable or valid and are totally dependent on the individual providing the reference. Most organizations will not give you information about past employees except to verify dates of employment, job title, and salary. As stated earlier, it would be inappropriate to contact a current employer without a candidate's permission, as it could jeopardize the individual's current employment.

8. *Drug testing.* Most companies do this because "everybody else does it." That is not a bad reason if you are in an industry where work accidents can occur. Organizations should always use experts, tell candidates early in the selection process, and do the testing after the choice has been made. Good tests are expensive.

9. *Physicals.* Physicals should be done only when there are job-related reasons to verify specific aspects of health and fitness. Often organizations use physicals when hiring at the senior level, since those types of jobs are highly stressful. You want to make sure that a candidate can handle the level of stress typical for the job. Always use an expert.

10. *Assessment centers.* Research has shown that assessment centers can be useful for predicting management and leadership ability. The centers should be developed by experts and validated prior to their use for

selection purposes. Typically, organizations use these centers to screen inside candidates for promotions to leadership positions.

An assessment center consists of a small group of candidates who are placed in a room together and given a series of job-related assignments. A panel of experts observes the interaction of the candidates and evaluates them based on a set of agreed-upon criteria. These criteria may include aspects like showing initiative, relating well to others, organizational skills, and communication skills. Assessment centers usually last from one to four days. When the assessment center is over, the panel develops a report with evaluative comments and suggestions for development for each candidate. Typically, employees who hope to move up in an organization participate in these centers and then work on the recommendations they are given so that they will be better qualified for future promotions.

I have repeatedly used the terms *valid* and *reliable* when talking about various selection tools. Let me explain each of the terms before we go further.

Validity of Selection Tools

Quite simply, validity means that the tool measures what it is supposed to measure. If you want to know if a candidate is conscientious, the test should accurately measure conscientiousness. If a structured interview question is intended to measure whether a candidate takes initiative in leadership situations, the question should measure that.

Three types of validity are important when using selection tools: content validity, criterion-related validity, and construct validity.

CONTENT VALIDITY

Does the selection accurately measure skills and abilities that are part of the job? In the case of a public speaking test, will the leader use the skills measured by the test on a regular basis on the job? If it is known that the leader will make frequent presentations to different groups, the test may be valid. If speeches are given once per year, on average, and involve nothing more than a brief report, the test is not valid. You also need to determine to whom the leader will be speaking. A speech to a small group of employees is quite different from a speech to 5,000 stockholders. The skills needed to deal with the former are quite different from the skills needed to deal with the latter. The test should simulate the actual work environment as closely as possible. This might mean that you attend a speech that each candidate makes in order to accurately assess his or her skill level.

CRITERION-RELATED VALIDITY

Does the test accurately predict job performance? Do leaders with high scores on a test of conscientiousness perform their jobs well? In other words, will leaders who scored higher do a better job one, five, and ten years later? There should be a direct and positive correlation between the test score and measures of performance over time. This type of validity can be established in two ways: concurrent validity and predictive validity.

CONCURRENT VALIDITY   The test is given to current leaders (without any preparation time allowed) and the score on the test should be positively correlated with existing measures of related work performance. Related performance measures may include profitability of a unit, performance appraisal ratings, sales records, or grievances filed. This type of selection tool validity can be established quickly as the performance records should already exist. Once the right range of scores is identified, it can be used for selection purposes.

PREDICTIVE VALIDITY   The test is given to all candidates for leadership positions, but not used for selection purposes currently. Later (one, two, and three years later), the score is compared to measures of work performance by leaders. The scores on the test should be positively correlated with measures of related work performance. This type of validity takes time to prove and requires a large number of new hires, something which is unusual for leadership positions, especially at the higher levels. Once validity is established, the test can be used for selection purposes.

CONSTRUCT VALIDITY

Does the test measure what it says it measures? If it is a speaking ability test, does it measure speaking ability or does it really measure friendliness? Or does it measure both? With a personality test, does it really measure the traits that are necessary for competent leaders? For example, if conscientiousness is important for successful leaders, does the test being used accurately measure that trait? A test must be validated prior to its use for selection purposes. Validity is a difficult thing to establish with leadership positions for one very big reason. There are so few leadership positions that it is hard to compare test results with actual performance. For large organizations, this is less of a problem. But the higher one goes up the corporate ladder, the fewer leadership positions can be found. Establishing criterion-related validity is more difficult. I recommend using testing centers that have data from across organizations. This way, leader attributes that cut across companies and industries can be measured and compared. This helps to better establish validity. If you use a testing center, they should provide information to you about the validity of any selection tool that they use.

Reliability

Reliability refers to the consistency of the test over candidates, assessors, and time. A reliable test or tool can be used by different decision makers and at different times with the same or similar results. This requires research on the selection tool that is beyond the ability of most individuals who make hiring decisions. When possible, only tests determined by experts to be reliable should be used. If you use a testing center, they should provide information to you about the reliability of any selection tool that they use.

Choosing the Right Selection Tool

Which selection tools are best for each attribute in each position on which we have been focusing? Let's take a look.

SCENARIO 1: PRESIDENT OF SUNSHINE FISHING CLUB

Realistically, you are probably not going to use any type of cognitive ability or personality testing for the president of a social club. The cost is too high and the level of expertise in this area is limited. A good structured interview may be your best tool. You may also want to look at samples of the individual's work in other organizations or in the club.

Structured interview for: Honesty, conscientiousness, optimism, friendliness, an interest in other people, emotional stability, likes fishing, good fishing skills, planning and organizing skills, handles large sums of money well, understanding of or willingness to learn the travel business. Minimal leadership experience.

SCENARIO 2: VICE PRESIDENT OF PLANNING FOR A FORTUNE 500 COMPANY

For this position, you should use a combination of selection tools. This is what I recommend:

Cognitive ability test for: Intelligence.

Personality test for: Conscientiousness, extroversion, optimism, energy level, future orientation, self-confidence, and persistence.

Work sample or performance test for: Computer skills, organizational skills, writing skills, business knowledge, knowledge of the industry and the law.

Structured interview for: Consistent values, positive attitude toward all aspects of business, initiative, participative style of leadership.

SCENARIO 3: HIGH SCHOOL PRINCIPAL

For this position, you should use a combination of selection tools. This is what I recommend:

Personality test for: Conscientiousness, extroversion, optimism, energy level, emotional stability, present oriented, persistence, and self-confidence.

Honesty test.

Structured interview for: Saltiness, leadership experience, family oriented, consistent values, positive attitude toward children, detail oriented, willing to constantly monitor performance data, considerate toward teachers and staff, and interpersonal skills.

Work sample or performance test: Knowledge of education, teaching, and administration.

SCENARIO 4: DIRECTOR OF PUBLIC RELATIONS FOR A HISTORICAL SOCIETY

For this position, you should use a combination of selection tools. This is what I recommend:

Personality test for: Conscientiousness, extroversion, friendliness, cooperativeness, optimism, high energy level, future oriented, and self-confidence.

Work sample or performance test for: Excellent writing skills, knowledge of the media and public relations, basic knowledge of and willingness to learn about the historical society, strong knowledge of marketing, advertising, and promotion.

Structured interview for: Consistent values, positive attitude about the value of the work of the society, ability to deal with frustration and ambiguity, interpersonal skills, influence skills, and creativity.

Scenario 5: Mayor of a Midsized City in the Rust Belt

Realistically, you are unlikely to be able to test candidates for any political office. However, you can obtain work samples by observing them, and you may be able to interview them by asking questions in public forums. These interviews will be unstructured at best. In practice, your "interviews" may be conducted by reporters and others during campaign visits.

Work samples and performance tests for: Friendliness, cooperativeness, optimism, speaking skills, high energy level.

Unstructured interview for: Organizational skills, understanding of or willingness to learn about local laws and government at all levels, influence skills, visionary, interpersonal skills, persistence, ability to deal with frustration and ambiguity, creativity, self-confidence, and willingness to travel and meet with corporate decision makers.

Scenario 6: CEO of a Large Urban Hospital

For this position, you should use a combination of selection tools. This is what I recommend:

Cognitive ability test for: Intelligence.

Personality test for: Conscientiousness, extroversion, future oriented, friendly, cooperative, optimism, energy level, persistence, self-confidence, and emotional stability.

Honesty test.

Work samples and performance tests for: Organizational skills, understanding of hospital administration and health care, knowledge of the law in the field, and influence skills.

Structured interview for: Respect for tradition, consistent values, positive attitude toward patients and health care professionals, initiative, visionary, considerate, strong interpersonal skills, and creativity.

SCENARIO 7: YOUR POSITION

Now, try this for the leadership position important to you.

Position title: _____

Cognitive ability test for: _____

_____

_____

Personality test for: _____

_____

_____

Work samples and performance tests for: _____

_____

_____

Structured interview for: _____

_____

_____

Using the selection tools we have identified, you should be able to determine the best-qualified candidate for each leadership position. As you can see, this is a very time-consuming task. Again, it is an investment. Now, let's learn how to develop and conduct a structured interview.

6 Developing and Conducting a Structured Interview

The interview is the most widely used selection tool in the United States. When the interview is structured, it has high validity (i.e., it contributes to our ability to predict future work performance) and reliability (i.e., it gives us consistent information over time with different candidates). A structured interview is a formal series of questions based on the position's required attributes or qualifications. The questions are asked of all candidates and evaluated using a predetermined measure. Unfortunately, most businesspeople use unstructured interviews. An unstructured interview is equivalent to a professor asking different students different exam questions unrelated to the material covered in a class. Unstructured interviews are neither valid nor reliable and often contain questions that could lead to lawsuits. They do not work. Developing a structured interview can be time consuming but becomes easier with practice.

Guide to Structured Interviews

Here is a step-by-step guide to developing and conducting a structured interview.

Step 1. Using the attributes or qualifications identified before recruiting began, the structured interview should be developed to gather information that will help select the best leader. Determine which skills can be best evaluated using an interview. For example, an interview is not the best way to determine whether someone can develop an engineering plan. An interview, however, can help you determine whether the candidate understands appropriate uses of specific engineering techniques. For each of the attributes you identified, a set of two to four questions must be developed.

Step 2. Use closed-ended questions to clear up any gaps in each candidate's work history, to identify names of past employers, to get the names of educational institutions, and to ask if the individual can deal with relevant working conditions. For example, "Your application says that you worked for Dr. Scott. What type of research does Dr. Scott do?" "I noticed that you have a five-year gap in your employment history. Where were you employed during that time?" "This job would require you to be on your feet most of the work day. Would that be a problem for you?" Ask only as many questions as necessary to gather the information you need. Much of this information should be gathered during the telephone recruiting meetings. You can save a great deal of time by prescreening.

Step 3. Use open-ended behavioral and situational interview questions to clarify less tangible performance skills. Ask at least one question of each type. It is preferable to ask three or four questions of either type. You are trying to identify a behavioral pattern. If you ask only one question for each skill, you may get the wrong answer. Two more questions may reveal different information about the applicant. Since people are typically nervous during an employment interview, the first answer may be related to stress rather than an accurate picture of the candidate's skills. You are looking for patterns.

Step 4. Behavioral interview questions have been empirically tested and produce valid results. These questions ask a candidate to reflect on and share past experiences and work performance. The candidate explains how he or she has performed in the past, which is a good indication of how he or she will behave when working for you. Please note that behavioral questions are no guarantee of honesty. However, they are rarely used. Therefore, people are not used to them. They often catch candidates off guard, and they are more likely to give you the real story. For more typical interview questions, candidates may have canned responses.

The following are some examples of behavioral interview questions. Note the skill being evaluated and the underlined phrases in each question.

Customer oriented: "Describe a time when you had to give a client bad news. Tell me how you did it."

Shows initiative: "Tell me about a situation when a problem occurred with a customer's bill and your boss was not around. What did you do?"

Teamwork: "Describe a situation in your current position when you had to get information from a number of different people. How did you get the information you needed on a timely basis?"

Handles stress well: "Think of a time when a difficult situation occurred with a project you were leading. Tell me about it. What did you do to alleviate the stress?"

Ability to solve technical problems: "Explain a situation in your current position when a piece of equipment used on the production floor broke down on a busy day. What did you do?"

Step 5. Situational interview questions have also been empirically tested and produce valid results. These questions ask a candidate to speculate on how he or she would deal with a hypothetical situation. The situations used for these questions should be real situations that have occurred in the past in your organization. People tend to accurately predict how they will perform and you can decide if that is what you want. Here are some examples. Note the underlined words.

Customer oriented: "Imagine that a customer in the restaurant you are managing spits out the food and begins swearing. What would you do?"

Shows initiative: "Suppose that the district manager is gone for the day and cannot be reached. A customer calls to say that he must talk to the district manager immediately. What would you do?"

Teamwork: "If you were assigned an administrative assistant whom you disliked, what would you do?"

Handles stress well: "If you had a very stressful morning before arriving at the office, what would you do to prepare yourself to deal with problems in the office?"

Ability to solve technical problems: "Pretend that your laptop broke down during an important presentation using PowerPoint slides. What would you do?"

Step 6. Review your questions to make sure that they are job related. Throw out any that are not. If the information you are gathering is not job related, it might provide reasons to discriminate against a good candidate or in favor of a bad candidate.

Do not ask personal questions about the candidates unless a question is specifically job related. When a personal characteristic is required for a job, it is called a bona fide occupational qualification (BFOQ). It is legal to ask personal questions if the BFOQ is valid. The skill or qualification must be job related or you may find yourself involved in a lawsuit. For example, if you need a Spanish speaker to head a unit working with bilingual customers, you may ask candidates if they speak Spanish. You should not ask if candidates learned to speak Spanish from their parents. What if you are hiring for a Catholic hospital? You should not ask if candidates are Catholic unless you are hiring a priest to supervise the counseling staff for Catholic patients and their families. In that case, religion may be a legitimate job qualification.

Do not ask about owning a car, having children, or marriage. Many people incorrectly assume that car owners are less likely to be late for work, mothers miss more work than nonmothers, and married men are more responsible at work than single men. Do not ask and you will not have to worry about your own biases (or, worse yet, a discrimination lawsuit).

Occasionally, candidates feel a need to be "totally honest," and they reveal information about themselves that you should not take into consideration when making a selection decision. When a candidate tells you more than you need to know, set it aside cognitively. That is, think about it and let it go in your mind. For example, if a candidate for director of marketing tells you that he is a recovering alcoholic, you cannot legally discriminate against him. Review his qualifications like all other candidates. If a candidate for vice president of accounting tells you that she is pregnant, you cannot legally discriminate against her. Even though you have a right to be concerned about her ability to do the job during her medical leave, you cannot refuse to hire her if she says that her pregnancy will not interfere with her work. Both revelations may cause you some concern about the candidate, but you cannot legally use the information to make a decision.

In rare situations, some candidates may tell you about past illegal activities. Although it is hard to believe, candidates do this on occasion. Sometimes, they may be telling a funny story about themselves from their younger days. In other cases, they may be trying to convince you that they understand the underdog. Either way, if someone chooses to give you information about previous unlawful behavior that occurred past the age of eighteen, end the selection process of this candidate after the interview. Revealing this type of information or bragging about illegal behavior shows a lack of judgment that you do not want or need in any leadership position.

Step 7. Determine the right answer to each question. You must know what you are looking for or you will not find it. For example, if you ask candidates how they have handled difficult customers in their current job, the right answer depends on what you need in the position you are filling. If you want a head nurse who has patience and handles difficult patients gently, the right answer would be, "I stopped, carefully explained what I was doing and why, and waited until he was calm." If you want a director of security who deals aggressively with customers involved in an argument, the right answer would be, "I gave him one warning and when he started yelling again, I escorted him to the exit."

The right answer is the yardstick by which you measure all candidates. You determine what the right answer is based on the philosophy of your organization and your beliefs and attitudes. On occasion, an interviewee may educate you about the best answer, but remember to give credit to other candidates for that answer as well.

Step 8. After the initial screening, you should interview three to five finalists who have the basic technical qualifications. Look over each candidate's application and resume (remember, a resume is an advertisement— take it with a grain of salt) and tailor the questions to each individual. The questions will remain basically the same, but instead of saying, for example, "Tell me about a time when you were working at your current job and such and such happened," you will say, "Tell me about a time when you were a department manager at Kmart and . . ."

Step 9. Decide how you will rate the candidates. I suggest a simple three-point system:

0. The candidate does not have the required attribute.
1. The candidate has the required attribute.
2. The candidate is superior in terms of the required attribute.

Step 10. Assign weights to the various attributes based on their importance for the position. Interpersonal skills are more important for a customer service manager than software skills. The opposite might be true for an accounting department manager. The easiest way to do this is to start with 100 points and distribute the points among the different skills based on their importance. You can then multiply your rating by the weight for each skill and compute a numerical score for each candidate after the interview. Be sure to include all of the attributes when you assign the weights, not just the ones for which the structured interview is used.

Depending on the scope of the position, you may find it easier to use 200 or 300 points. For example, for a CEO position with many attributes, using 200 points may make it easier to distribute points. The number will not affect the outcome of the selection decision. Divide the points among the various attributes, giving the most points to the most important at- tributes for the position.

All of the individuals involved in the process should come up with their own estimates of how the points should be distributed. Then the group should meet and negotiate the final weights.

Step 11. Plan each interview carefully. Give the candidates sufficient notice. Try to schedule the meeting at their convenience. Make sure they know how to reach your location and where to park. Make sure they are greeted in a courteous and professional manner. You have to impress them—you want the best people to want to work for you. Besides, you never know when one of the candidates might become a customer. Sched- ule enough time for the interview, time to make notes afterward, and time to evaluate the candidate after the interview ends.

Step 12. The following is a good procedure to follow when conducting interviews.

1. Welcome the candidate and introduce yourself and other inter- viewers.
2. Make a little small talk and offer a beverage to put the person at ease.
3. Explain the interview format and why you will take notes.
4. Clarify the background data using closed-ended questions.
5. Probe using the behavioral and situational interview questions.
6. Take good notes, even if you have to pause for a few seconds while you write.
7. Invite the candidate to ask questions about the job and the or- ganization.
8. Tell the candidate when a decision will be made and when the candidate can expect to hear from you (and stick with the time

frame or call the candidate to explain). If another interview or test is required, tell the candidate and schedule it after the interview. Whenever possible, do all of the screening at one time.

9. Thank the applicant for taking the time to come in.

Step 13. As you conduct the interview, give the candidates time to think about their answers. When you ask more complicated open-ended questions about their past experiences, it takes longer to think about answers and formulate responses.

Step 14. If more than one person will make the decision about which candidate to hire, it makes sense to have two to three people interview each candidate at one time. This is called panel interviewing. Research has shown that this approach can improve the reliability of an interview. The panel must be the same for each candidate. Responsibility for developing the questions can be shared after the attributes have been identified and agreed upon. Following the interview, the interviewers should evaluate the candidate together.

Step 15. When evaluating a candidate after the interview, you will use the information reported by the candidate and observations that you made during the interview. Do not use information that is not related to the job or make conclusions that you cannot substantiate. In your notes, provide specific useful information like this: "She demonstrated a system of monitoring course scheduling." Do not write, "She showed know-how." Say, "He asked detailed questions about safety equipment and procedures in effect," not "Seems cautious."

After interviewing three applicants, the candidates may begin to look alike. Do not write down notes that are irrelevant such as, "He is single," or "She has kids." If you ever find yourself involved in a discrimination lawsuit, your interview notes will be either your best defense or incriminating evidence. Keep your notes and make sure the evaluative comments are job related, professional, and useful to you.

Step 16. Get rid of inappropriate questions commonly asked in interviews. For example: What book have you read lately? Who is the leader you most admire? What are your weaknesses? Questions like these have nothing to do with most jobs and can lead to biases. For example, if a person says that he admires George W. Bush, you would assume that he is a Republican, which could create a bias either for or against the candidate.

If a person says that the most recent book she has read is *Left Behind*, you might make assumptions about her religion. These kinds of questions have no value to the selection process and can actually create problems.

Step 17. Plan how you will promote your organization during the interview process. You can do this by providing tours, introducing the candidates to key individuals, treating all candidates professionally and kindly in every aspect of the selection process, providing comfortable space for testing, answering all questions, providing a realistic preview of job responsibilities, and offering a high-quality meal when appropriate. In addition, you must talk about the advantages of the position. For example, you may offer good pay, benefits, contribution to the community or friends, fun work, collegial organization, nice working conditions, influence and power, the chance to accomplish personal or professional goals, and the opportunity to meet lots of people. You must sell the leadership position. Even if you do not pay the most (or at all), the leadership position in your organization can be the best. Consider giving the candidates printed information that highlights the strengths of the organization.

Other Considerations and Wrapping Up the Process

The Source of Leadership Behavior and Implications for Selection

Research and anecdotal evidence suggest that managers and leaders learn to lead by observing their own past leaders. This means that even the best-educated leader will be influenced and shaped by vicarious experiences. From the standpoint of choosing the right leaders, it is important to ask about a leader who influenced a candidate. Ask about the style of leadership that individual used, and how the candidate has adopted, adapted, or rejected that style. This can be done during the structured interview process. The following are some questions that could be used for every interview for a leadership position:

1. Tell me about a previous leader with whom you have worked who stands out in your mind.

2. What was that person's leadership style?

3. What did you like or dislike about that style?

4. Tell me how your leadership style has been influenced by that leader.

5. What aspects of that leader's behavior have you adopted or adapted to fit your own personal style?

6. What aspects of that leader's behavior have you rejected and why?

Research on Interviewing

Here are fifteen interviewing tips based on what Campion, Palmer, and Campion found in their review of published empirical work on selection interviews.[1] These tips should enhance the reliability and validity of the interview and improve reactions by job candidates.

1. Base your interview questions on the job analysis (or job description).

2. Ask the same questions of every candidate, tailoring them to each candidate's past experience.

3. Limit prompting of candidates, follow-up questioning, and elaboration on questions that may inadvertently solicit the right answers to interview questions.

4. Use types of questions (situational, behavioral, background, and job-knowledge questions) that have been empirically tested.

5. Use a long interview and many questions, at least three per attribute.

6. Control the impact of ancillary information (e.g., applications, resumes, transcripts, etc.). A well-designed resume (e.g., format, paper quality, color) can bias you even when the content (e.g., experience and education) is no better or worse than another candidate's.

7. Do not allow questions from a candidate until after your questions have been answered.

8. Rate each answer carefully.

9. Use detailed anchored rating scales based on the right answer.

10. Take detailed notes during the interview.

11. Use two to three interviewers.
12. Use the same interviewers for all candidates even when it is inconvenient.
13. Do not discuss candidates or their answers between interviews.
14. Provide extensive interviewing training in your organization.
15. Use quantitative rather than clinical predictions of performance.

Hiring the Best Candidate

Put all of the information that you have gathered together. Keep in mind which attributes are most important. Remember that some technical skills can be taught. Compare each candidate on each tool used in your strategy. Which candidate received the highest scores on each tool? Which did best overall?

Chances are that if you did the recruiting and the initial screening well, you may have two candidates who look equally well qualified. You must now use your judgment to make the final decision. Here are some questions to ask yourself as you consider your choices:

- Which leader candidate complements the staff that you currently have?
- Does one candidate have a special skill, expertise, or characteristic (for example, a second language) that would add value to the organization?
- Did one of the candidates offend you or others during the selection process?
- Did one of the candidates make you or others feel particularly comfortable during the interview?
- Are you sure that your comfort level with a candidate is not based on gender, race, ethnicity, religion, former college, neighborhood where the candidate grew up, or some such information? If so, this comfort level is not a valid predictor of job performance. Put these biases aside and think about job-related criteria.

Chapter 7 includes a large set of interview questions for the six scenarios explored in this book. You should find these questions helpful when you begin to write your own interview questions.

Structured Interview Questions

This chapter includes examples of questions that could be used to interview candidates for the six positions described in the sample scenarios. I have also provided examples of best answers. Keep in mind that only the people making the selections know the right answers for their organizations. These samples show the types of responses an organization might find preferable. Perhaps some of these questions and answers will also work in your organization. I have provided many in the hope that readers will be able to use them.

Each attribute is listed for each scenario, followed by a set of behavioral questions and their right answers. Then situational questions and their right answers are listed.

Scenario 1: President of Sunshine Fishing Club

Honesty

Behavioral interview question: Describe a situation where you observed a coworker doing something unethical. What did you do?

Right answer: I asked him what he was doing and why. I asked him to stop or return the items he had taken.

Behavioral interview question: Tell me about a time when you knew a friend was cheating on a test or an assignment at work. How did you handle it?

Right answer: I did not participate and told her that I did not think it was right.

Situational interview question: Suppose that someone in the club asked you to loan him money from the fishing trip fund to help with a family emergency. What would you do?

Right answer: The right answer may vary depending on the past practices of the club, but you probably want to discuss this request with the membership of the group. If they say it is OK, you can do it. Otherwise, you want the interviewee to say no to the request.

Situational interview question: If a travel agent offered to discount your family's trip to Disney World next summer if you choose their agency to arrange the club's fishing trip, what would you do and why?

Right answer: I would say no, even if it did not cost the club any additional money, because the conflict of interest may be interpreted as unethical by some club members.

Conscientiousness

Behavioral interview question: Tell me about a time when you had more work than you could handle in your work day. How did you handle it?

Right answer: I stayed late and got it done.

Behavioral interview question: Describe a time when you had a lot of work to do at home and a friend asked you to go fishing. What did you do?

Right answer: I did the work. (If a candidate went fishing when he or she had work to do at home, that candidate will probably go fishing instead of taking care of the club's business.)

Situational interview question: If you were faced with a decision of spending a weekend fishing with friends or helping your child's school with a fund-raising project, how would you decide which activity to do?

Right answer: I would assess the value of the fund-raiser. If it was only raising $100, everyone would be better off if I just gave the money. If it was a necessary fund-raising event that would raise thousands of dollars for a special program that I supported, I would participate in the fund-raiser on the weekend. (You are interested in the thought process in this situation. Was the decision made carefully and conscientiously?)

Situational interview question: If a member of the fishing club told you that he was going on the trip and then cancelled at the last minute, demanding his money back because something better came up, how would you handle it?

Right answer: I would refund the money and advise him that the money would not be refunded the next time it happens.

Optimism

Behavioral interview question: Think about a time when you were working with someone who had a negative attitude. Tell me about it and how you handled the situation.

Right answer: A colleague told me that he did not get a promotion and he was complaining about management. I tried to remain positive myself and refused to engage in the negative discussion.

Behavioral interview question: Tell me about a difficult time at your job recently. How did you deal with it?

Right answer: We had a big decrease in orders and several coworkers were laid off. I was very worried but made it a point to try a little harder so that the products would be good and hopefully lead to more orders.

Situational interview question: If you had a couple of club members who always worried about the worst case scenario for every trip you planned, what would you do?

Right answer: I would anticipate their attitudes and head off their concerns with lots of information and details about each trip.

Situational interview question: Imagine that during one of the trips you planned, it rained every single day. What would you do? Be specific.

Right answer: I would always plan for alternate activities that would appeal to people who like to fish. For example, I would find out how to arrange a bus tour of a wildlife preserve in the area.

Friendliness

Behavioral interview question: On your last fishing trip with the club, how many people did you meet for the first time? How did you go about meeting new people?

Right answer: I met several people at the bait shop who gave me some tips on the best locations. I talk easily to others and interact with all club members.

Behavioral interview question: How many club members do you see outside of the fishing trips? What do you do?

Right answer: Several of us get together with our families on a regular basis. (Friendly people have numerous friendships, which are likely to extend to other aspects of their lives.)

Situational interview question: If you entered a fishing resort on a trip by yourself, how would you meet people?

Right answer: I would talk to the manager, eat in the dining room, check to see if anyone was looking for a fishing partner the next day, and stop at the pub in the evening.

Situational interview question: Imagine that a new club member seems a bit shy and rarely talks to other members. What would you do to help her make friends?

Right answer: I would introduce her to several of the members who are outgoing. I would encourage her to attend the annual group trips.

Emotional Stability

Behavioral interview question: Tell me about a time when you were upset about something that happened at work. How did you handle it?

Right answer: I went fishing after work. (What you are looking for is someone who has developed coping strategies for dealing with stress and pressure.)

Behavioral interview question: Describe a time when someone tried to pick a fight with you. What did you do?

Right answer: I refused to engage in any name calling or to raise my voice. I tried to address concerns logically and be respectful of the other person.

Situational interview question: Imagine that you have encountered some problems with the upcoming fishing trip. What will you do?

Right answer: I will calmly take it one step at a time, working on each problem. I will ask for help.

Situational interview question: If someone in the club questioned the way you handled the money for a big trip, what would you do?

Right answer: I would get a copy of the trip budget with all numbers broken down and the costs documented. I would share that with the person who was concerned.

Likes Fishing and Has Good Fishing Skills

Open-ended question: Tell me how long you have been fishing and why you enjoy it.

Right answer: I have been fishing for many years. It helps me relax and it is exciting.

Closed-ended question: What types of fishing have you done and where have you done it?

Right answer: (The right answer should include the types of fishing that the club most often does.)

Ask a series of closed-ended questions about specific skills that a good angler should have.

Right answer: (The right answers, of course!)

Planning and Organizing Skills

Behavioral interview question: Describe a time when you had a lot of tasks to perform in a limited amount of time. How did you get the most important tasks done?

Right answer: I prioritized the things I had to do and worked on the most important things first.

Behavioral interview question: Explain a situation at work when you were in charge of a project or assignment that involved others. How did you organize the group?

Right answer: I held a meeting where we discussed what had to be accomplished. The tasks were divided among the group and deadlines were set. I followed up with each person to check on progress.

Situational interview question: If you were selected as president of the club, how would you organize the expenses of the big annual fishing trip?

Right answer: I would keep detailed records of all payments and give each member receipts for payments. I would present a budget to the members and answer all questions honestly.

Situational interview question: If a particular trip offered several options for the members, how would you keep track of the preferences of each person?

Right answer: I would create a graph that would list all of the options available on each day with the names of all members across the top. As members made their reservations and their choices, I would put an X in the boxes and give everyone a copy to verify the information.

Handling Large Sums of Money Well

Behavioral interview question: Think of a time when you handled a large amount of money. How did you keep it straight?

Right answer: I kept good records and made daily deposits of the money. I verified the information with each person and gave written receipts.

Behavioral interview question: Tell me about a time when you had to coordinate finances on a project. How did you do it?

Right answer: I made detailed records of how much each person or department paid, the balance owed, and used receipts. I documented every penny.

Situational interview question: Suppose that you had planned a trip and a member came to you at the last minute claiming to have paid. If your records did not show a payment, what would you do?

Right answer: I would request the original receipt. I would always use receipts and would have told everyone in the information about the trip that they would and should get and keep receipts.

Situational interview question: Imagine that you planned a trip for fifty people. What would you do to guarantee that all of the records were accurate?

Right answer: I would create a computer spreadsheet for each expense item and track every dime spent and taken in. I would have a second person check my records on a regular basis to ensure accuracy and integrity in the process.

Understanding of or Willingness to Learn the Travel Business

Behavioral interview question: Tell me about a time when you planned a trip for your family or friends. How did you go about it?

Right answer: I researched the types of locations that we were interested in visiting, gathered data on travel and hotel rates, and presented the information to the group.

Behavioral interview question: Describe a situation when something went wrong while on a vacation. How did you handle it?

Right answer: My son got sick. We thought it was an ear infection. We went to the owner of the lodge where we were staying and got the name of the local clinic. I took my son and got the necessary prescription.

Situational interview question: If you planned a trip with the club and the fishing lodge where you were going burned to the ground one week before, what would you do?

Right answer: I would immediately file for the travel insurance that I would have obtained for the members. I would notify the members that the trip would be postponed and the reasons. I would then begin researching an alternate hotel or lodge in the same location, keeping the members fully informed throughout the process. My goal would be to go ahead with the trip as scheduled.

Situational interview question: If the members chose a location with which you were not familiar, what would you do?

Right answer: I would go online and find information at the library or through travel agents about the location.

Minimal Leadership Experience

Behavioral interview question: Describe a time when you were asked to lead a project or a group. How did you begin?

Right answer: At work, I was asked to set up a project team to reduce production costs. I arranged a meeting of all concerned individuals and gathered all of the information I could get about the people and what my job was.

Behavioral interview question: Tell me about a situation when you were leading a team and a problem occurred. How did you handle it?

Right answer: I was working on a project at work and we found out that we did not have the necessary equipment for the job. I talked to coworkers and discussed the future needs of the project. Then I approached my boss with a complete list of needed equipment with a projected timeline.

Situational interview question: If you were leading a meeting of the fishing club and an argument broke out, how would you handle it?

Right answer: I would use humor to defuse the situation and then give each person a few minutes to explain his or her point of view. I would then ask other members to express their views and seek a compromise.

Situational interview question: If you had to form a special committee to look into a fishing opportunity for the club, how would you select the members of the committee?

Right answer: I would go to the most active members who have shown a special interest or past experience in the type of fishing being explored and ask them to serve on the committee.

Scenario 2: Vice President of Planning for a Fortune 500 Company

Consistent Values

Behavioral interview question: Think about a time when you had an opportunity to obtain a kickback from a supplier of goods or services. Tell me about it and explain how you handled it.

Right answer: An ad agency offered me a week-long vacation in Cancun while we were negotiating a deal. I refused and told them that it was inappropriate for them to make the offer. I informed my contact that future offers of that type would be considered bribes and would be cause to discontinue doing business with the agency. I informed my boss about it and documented the situation in writing.

Behavioral interview question: Tell me about your current community service activities. Why are you involved in them?

Right answer: I serve on the board of the YMCA and I am a Big Brother. I enjoy interacting with community groups. I meet new and interesting people. I also do it because I feel that it is my civic duty to participate in my community.

Situational interview question: If you were asked to serve on a project that was outside of your corporate responsibilities and would take you away from your core job tasks, what would you do?

Right answer: I would refuse the additional project but would offer to assist or consult with the team when I had the time to do so.

Situational interview question: If you were in a business meeting and were asked to describe your business philosophy, what would you say?

Right answer: I would say that my goal in business is to provide a good return for stockholders while holding high ethical and legal standards. I believe that strong moral business practices lead to higher earnings, a better workforce, and more satisfied customers.

Positive Attitude Toward All Aspects of Business

Behavioral interview question: Describe a time when you had problems working with a particular department. How did you resolve the problem?

Right answer: In my current job, I had a problem with an accounting manager who delayed sending checks to suppliers. The process that the department had in place had so many safeguards that it was inefficient. I had a face-to-face meeting with the manager. My approach was to talk about how the process could be expedited. He began to review his departmental procedures and made changes that cut one week off the accounts payable process. (Note that the approach was constructive rather than destructive toward another departmental manager.)

Behavioral interview question: In your current job, which departments do you usually work with most often, and why?

Right answer: As a planning executive, I must focus on the overall corporate goals. That means that every department is important to getting my job done well. I frequently interact with senior executives, but also deal with departmental managers at every level.

Situational interview question: If you got this job and found that one department in our company has poor management, how would you work with those managers to develop an effective plan?

Right answer: I would educate the management team about planning and show them the advantages to learning to do it well. I would train them on the basic aspects of planning while providing the tools to make it efficient.

Situational interview question: Unlike your current employer, our company has a research department. What would you do to learn our business and how we research and develop?

Right answer: I would attend corporate training programs as well as take additional classes outside of the company about this industry. I would also spend long hours observing the research labs, talking with customers, and getting to understand the function of every department.

Initiative

Behavioral interview question: Tell me about a time when you had to make a tough decision with broad consequences for the company and your supervisor was not around. How did you make the decision?

Right answer: I had to choose the supplier for a major resource used in our production. The decision came up unexpectedly for several unanticipated reasons. I carefully researched the options and discussed the decision with my peers. I made the final decision based on what I perceived as best for the organization.

Behavioral interview question: In your current job, think of a time when you were called and asked for an opinion that was needed immediately. How did you handle it?

Right answer: This happened recently. I was asked if the company should continue working with an ad agency. I refused to give an immediate answer. I quickly gathered data on the relationship between sales and the various recent ad campaigns. Within four hours, I gave a response.

Situational interview question: If your boss put you in charge while she was out of the country, what strategy would you use to make decisions?

Right answer: I would gather information and then make firm decisions. I am not afraid to stick my neck out and admit later if I have made a mistake. Unless people could be harmed, I am very assertive about decisions.

Situational interview question: Suppose that you believe your superior has made a very big mistake. What would you do?

Right answer: I would go to her immediately and explain my point of view. Unless the mistake could lead to legal problems for the company, in which case I would talk with legal counsel, I would support the final decision of my manager.

Participative Style of Leadership

Behavioral interview question: Tell me about a time when you were assigned a new project while you were the director of marketing for XYZ. How did you approach the assignment?

Right answer: I pulled my team together to discuss the project and to solicit their input.

Behavioral interview question: Describe your interaction with your subordinates in your current position.

Right answer: I work with my staff members on a daily basis. I value their ideas and frequently seek their opinions. I try to develop my staff and include them in decision making.

Situational interview question: If a subordinate came to you with an idea for a new approach to planning, what would you do and why?

Right answer: I would listen and seek additional information. I would study the proposal carefully and involve my staff in the decision on whether to try the new approach.

Situational interview question: Assume that you have been assigned to work on the plan for a new division of the corporation. What would you do first?

Right answer: I would talk to my staff and the management team of the division.

Scenario 3: High School Principal

Saltiness

Behavioral interview question: Tell me about a time when a student pulled a fast one on you. How did you deal with that?

Right answer: A student convinced me that he was in study hall when he was reported out of a gym class. I laughed when I realized my mistake. I found the student and confronted him with it. I used appropriate disciplinary action.

Behavioral interview question: Describe a situation when a parent pulled a fast one on you. How did you deal with that?

Right answer: I found out that a parent brought a sick child to school after being told by their family doctor that the child was contagious and should not be in school. I called the parent and expressed empathy for having to find care for a sick child when she had to work. I offered some suggestions for sick child care programs in our community.

Situational interview question: If one of the teachers in the school repeatedly called in sick, how would you handle it?

Right answer: I would schedule a meeting with the teacher. I would let him or her know that absences are a problem for the school and the children in class. I would talk with him or her about the reasons for the absences. If I had a clue that something else was in play, like a drinking problem, for example, I would directly address that issue and offer assistance. I would be very careful to outline consequences of further absences.

Situational interview question: Imagine that you found a male student hiding in the girls' locker room hoping to take a digital picture of the girls changing to put on the Internet. You caught him before he took the photo. What would you do?

Right answer: I would confront him and explain the consequences if the photo had been taken and placed on the Internet. I would administer the appropriate discipline. I would find a suitable substitute for the talents and interests of the student.

Leadership Experience

Behavioral interview question: Tell me about a time when you were part of a group without a formal leader. What role did you play?

Right answer: In my civic club, we do not have officers. We volunteer to lead projects that we care about. I initiated a fund-raiser for the local school athletic program and led a group of interested members. We raised $5,000.

Behavioral interview question: In your current job, describe a program that you initiated. How did you accomplish your goals?

Right answer: I began the After-School Activities Program. We know that teens are more apt to get into trouble after school than at other times. I began a series of activities for kids that began when school let out and lasted for two hours. I worked with individual teachers who were willing to organize activities related to their interests outside of work.

Situational interview question: If you were asked to head a system-wide project, how would you approach it?

Right answer: I would find others in the system with an interest in the subject of the project. I would meet with them individually to determine their level of interest and opinions on how the program should be structured and run. I would then form a committee, delegate responsibility for various pieces of the project, and serve as the co-ordinator. I would represent the committee when proposals had to be taken to administrators or the school board.

Situational interview question: If a problem occurred with a program that you managed, what would you do?

Right answer: I would take responsibility for the problems, attempt to determine the causes of the problem, and try to either fix it or make necessary changes so the program goals would be achieved.

Family Oriented

Behavioral interview question: Describe a situation when a student had to miss school due to a family emergency. What did you do?

Right answer: I had a student whose father was injured in a serious accident. The student had to care for younger children and could not attend school for one week. I gathered his schoolwork from teachers, delivered it to his home, and later collected the completed assignments. I also coordinated a group of volunteers to provide meals for the family.

Behavioral interview question: Tell me about a time when you had a conflict between your family and your job. How did you resolve it?

Right answer: One of my children had a doctor's appointment that could not be rescheduled. I went to my boss, explained the situation, and took my child to the doctor. I made up the time later.

Situational interview question: Suppose that a student has gotten into trouble at school and that the prescribed punishment is after-school detention. However, you know that this student works after school to help out his family financially. What will you do?

Right answer: I will work out an alternative like detention before school.

Situational interview question: Suppose that a particular program has always been held in the afternoons. However, a parent calls you and requests that it be moved to the evening so that working parents can attend. What will you do?

Right answer: I will change the program to evenings so that more parents can attend.

Consistent Values

See the questions from scenario 2 and use wording that fits an educational environment.

Positive Attitude Toward Children

Behavioral interview question: Tell me about the best time in your teaching career.

Right answer: When I taught seventh grade math and the students finally understood a difficult subject, I felt the best about my teaching and its effect on the children. (Note that the answer should include positive interaction with children.)

Behavioral interview question: Describe a difficult disciplinary problem you had with a child. How did you deal with it?

Right answer: I caught a girl cheating on a test. I talked to her about why she did it. I worked with her to help her prepare for a different exam. She took it over her recess a few days later. She did well and was more confident that she could perform well without cheating.

Situational interview question: Imagine that a teacher comes to you and says that she has an impossible class—the students are "dumb" and behave poorly. What will you do?

Right answer: I will look at the assignment of students to ensure that she does not have an unusual number of problem students. If not, I will work with her on developing a more positive attitude about students and how to present a positive image to the kids. I will offer to visit the classroom to teach a few lessons and set an example of how to deal positively with difficult students.

Situational interview question: If a student called you a name, what would you do?

Right answer: I would take the appropriate disciplinary action and I would think about the reasons for the negative reaction. If the student had a right to be angry at me, I would adjust my behavior in the future.

Detail Oriented

Behavioral interview question: Think of a time when you were in charge of a highly detailed report. Tell me about it and how you ensured accuracy.

Right answer: I was responsible for reporting standardized test scores for the students in our school to the board. I carefully proofed the document and then asked a colleague with good proofing skills to check my work.

Behavioral interview question: Tell me about a situation where you made a mistake on some data. How did you handle the error?

Right answer: My boss found an error on a budget memo that I had written. I was very embarrassed and corrected the memo immediately, rechecking every number on the report with the finance manager.

Situational interview question: Suppose that you are asked to coordinate the budget for all of the schools in the district. What steps will you take to ensure accuracy?

Right answer: I will coordinate with the finance manager of the district, each of the principals, and the superintendent and her staff. I will check the sources of all data and have a person who is good with detail as part of the process.

Situational interview question: Imagine that you find a small, but important, mistake that another administrator has made. To point it out may bring embarrassment to that administrator. What will you do?

Right answer: I will contact the administrator directly and show him the error, thereby giving him an opportunity to "find" it himself and have it corrected. If it is not changed, I will report the mistake to the appropriate school official.

Willing to Constantly Monitor Performance Data

Behavioral interview question: In your current job, how did you follow up on standardized test scores when the school received them? Give a specific example.

Right answer: We received the state assessment scores in October. As soon as the scores were received, I reviewed them in detail. I provided copies to the superintendent and the teachers with my comments within a few days. I asked for feedback from them.

Behavioral interview question: In the situation you described above, what program changes were made? Be specific and provide an example.

Right answer: We had lower scores in reading comprehension for third graders than we had hoped, based on the previous year's test scores. I met with the reading specialists and we reviewed the scores for each student and teacher. We found that the scores were lower in the classroom of the new third grade teacher. I worked with the teacher and the reading specialist to improve the reading comprehension teaching methods that she was using.

Situational interview question: If you had the opportunity to skip the standardized testing for one year, would you do it? Why or why not?

Right answer: I would not skip the testing because it gives us valuable information that we need to improve our teaching methods and to identify children who need help.

Situational interview question: If your school had very bad results in just one year, what would you do?

Right answer: I would review the reports very carefully to see if there was a problem or if the results were a fluke. If it appears that it was just one off year, I would not panic. However, I would carefully review the next year's results for a developing pattern.

Considerate Toward Teachers and Staff

Behavioral interview question: Describe a time in your current job when one of the teachers had a personal problem. What did you do?

Right answer: Last year, one of the teachers lost her husband to cancer. I organized a support group that regularly called her, invited her to dinner, and included her in activities. We have maintained this group and it has brought our entire faculty closer together.

Behavioral interview question: Tell me about a time when you had to talk with a teacher about poor performance. How did you do it?

Right answer: A new teacher was having classroom control problems and it was disrupting that entire wing of the school. I went to her classroom at the end of a school day. I asked her about how things were going and she brought up the disciplinary problems she was having. We talked about some strategies that she could use. I followed up a couple of times a week for two months after that and eventually she got control.

Situational interview question: Suppose that you are in a hurry and need to have an office assistant make some copies. She wants to talk to you on another matter. What will you do?

Right answer: I will explain that I have a meeting and schedule a time within the next twenty-four hours to talk to her.

Situational interview question: If you had a student who was coming to school with bad body odor, what would you do?

Right answer: I would call the parents and let them know. If there was some problem in the home that precluded better grooming, I would ask the school nurse to get involved.

Interpersonal Skills

Behavioral interview question: Give me an example of a time when you had a conflict with a coworker. How did you handle it?

Right answer: I disagreed with my principal once on how to deal with a disruptive student. We discussed it and agreed to disagree on the solution to the issue. Since he was in charge, he had the final say, however. When it was over, we both moved on and dropped the matter.

Behavioral interview question: Talk about a recent meeting that you called. How did you do it?

Right answer: I called a meeting to discuss a change in the duty schedule. I told the teachers the reason that a change had to be made and what would happen if we did not change. I asked for their input and for ideas of how the change should be made. I then used their ideas to develop the new schedule, which we each reviewed before it was adopted.

Situational interview question: If a parent called you swearing and complaining, what would you do?

Right answer: I would loudly say that I would not talk unless the parent stopped swearing and yelling. If the parent continued, I would hang up.

Situational interview question: If a child was crying in the hallway during school, what would you do?

Right answer: I would ask the child to join me in the library and talk with him to find out what was wrong. I think that a library is a better place to talk because it is less threatening than a principal's office.

Scenario 4: Director of Public Relations for a Historical Society

Consistent Values

See the questions from scenario 3 and use wording that fits a public agency.

Positive Attitude about the Value of the Work of the Society

Behavioral interview question: Think of a time in your current job when you were questioned about the value of the work done by your organization. How did you handle it?

Right answer: I was asked how I could justify spending $10 million on historical education when people were hungry. I explained that history helps us predict future events leading to hunger and that if we studied and applied our learning more, poverty could decrease.

Behavioral interview question: Tell me why you decided to take your current job.

Right answer: I have always read and studied history in my spare time and this job gives me the opportunity to merge my avocation with my professional talents.

Situational interview question: Suppose that a group of legislators has given you five minutes to present your most compelling argument for continued funding of the historical society. What would your first response be?

Right answer: I would tell them that research shows that the best way to predict the future is by understanding our past.

Situational interview question: If you were asked by a television commentator to explain the value of having a state historical agency, what would you say?

Right answer: I would respond that history is a very complex subject and that by studying the history of each state, we develop a better understanding.

Ability to Deal with Frustration and Ambiguity

Behavioral interview question: Explain a situation when you had to deal with a problem that was outside of your control. How did you handle it?

Right answer: An agency where I worked previously had a scandal that hit the media. The married director was having an affair with a high school–age tour guide. My primary goal when talking to the press was to distance the director's behavior from the work of the agency. I was honest in my answers and proactive in keeping the media apprised of the actions taken by the agency's board.

Behavioral interview question: Talk about a time when a reporter called requesting an interview, but would not say what the interview was about. How did you prepare?

Right answer: A reporter from the largest local newspaper called and asked to talk with me two months ago. All he would say was that he needed to run some things by me. I reviewed all recent announcements and press releases out of our organization for the past two weeks. I made sure that the director did not know of any breaking news. When he arrived, it turned out that he wanted to apply for the job of communications director.

Situational interview question: If you were to get a question from the media regarding the personal behavior of an employee, what would you do?

Right answer: I would respond that the personal behavior of our employees is just that—personal. I would further say that if a law had been broken, the agency would address the situation when and if the employee was convicted. Obviously, this would depend on the severity of the charges.

Situational interview question: If our agency makes a groundbreaking discovery, how would you announce the findings?

Right answer: I would plan a major media event. The appropriate reporters from all over the United States would be invited to attend a press conference. A series of press conferences, demonstrations, and displays would be prepared to accompany the release.

Interpersonal Skills

See the questions from scenario 3 and use wording that fits a public agency.

Influence Skills

Behavioral interview question: Describe a time when you had to sell an idea to your boss. Tell me how you did it.

Right answer: I wanted to begin using television advertising, which is very expensive. I put together facts that I gathered from comparable agencies about the effect of TV advertising on their visitations and contributions. I took this data to the director, who agreed to try advertising on a trial basis.

Behavioral interview question: Talk about a time when you raised funds for your agency from a private donor. How did you approach it?

Right answer: I invited the prospective donor to the museum after hours with his family. We prepared a special light show and tour highlighting the ongoing work of our historians. We left blank spaces in the tour that showed the work that had yet to be done. In each space was a dollar figure showing the amount of money needed to fund that particular study. It was very effective. The donor chose the study he was most interested in and fully funded it.

Situational interview question: If you had to convince a reporter to not run a damaging story about the society, how would you do it?

Right answer: If the story was legitimate news, I would not try to stop the reporter. If it was simply destructive gossip, I would offer to provide leads on better stories in the future.

Situational interview question: If you had to prepare an informational brochure that would be given to legislators before they voted on funding for the agency, what would you do?

Right answer: The brochure would be clean, accurate, well designed, and obviously inexpensive to produce. I would point out the accomplishments of the society and link those to tangible outcomes for state citizens.

Creativity

Behavioral interview question: Think of a time when you had to hold a banquet for the media. What did you do?

Right answer: We had the event in the historical village and served foods that came from the time frame represented by the village. The media representatives were invited to bring their families and the event was done as an educational activity.

Behavioral interview question: Please tell me about the brochure that you developed to attract visitors to the new historical site.

Right answer: The brochure featured photographs of the buildings at the new site. When the brochure was opened, it appeared that one had opened the door to a log cabin and walked inside. The brochure also included a link to a Web site that provided detailed information about visiting the site.

Situational interview question: If the director of the society asked for a new idea for the annual board meeting, how would you develop a creative idea?

Right answer: I like to use a clustering technique. I would put the project name in the center of a large piece of paper and use a web of links to each aspect of the project. I would then create a list of statements that begin with the phrase, "Wouldn't it be great if...?" I would use those statements to drive my thinking and planning.

Situational interview question: If a staff member came to you with a creative idea for a new educational program, how would you judge its value?

Right answer: I would test the idea with a sample of visitors to the society. If it worked with them, I would expand the program.

Scenario 5: Mayor of a Midsized City in the Rust Belt

Organizational Skills

Behavioral interview question: Tell me about a time when you had to coordinate a major project. How did you do it?

Right answer: I had to develop a proposal for a new housing development. I used a matrix to structure the projects with a cascade of reporting lines that ended on my desk. I met with each of the departmental managers involved twice per week. I read every report.

Behavioral interview question: What changes did you make when you took your current job?

Right answer: I assessed the importance and value of each position reporting to me. I reorganized so that there were fewer levels and so that reporting was done directly to me by each first-line supervisor. I eliminated five unnecessary positions.

Situational interview question: If you wanted to make sure that each function was done well, what would you do?

Right answer: I would assess the skill level of each employee in each position. If there were performance gaps, they would be corrected through training and education. If the incumbent could not perform the job, that person would be replaced.

Situational interview question: How would you schedule your work time in this position?

Right answer: I would prioritize the tasks that needed to be done each day and schedule the most important things first. Less important activities might be delegated to others or put back to another day or week.

Understanding of or Willingness to Learn about Local Laws and Government at All Levels

Behavioral interview question: Tell me about a time when you had to learn detailed new information. How did you go about that?

Right answer: When I won my current position, I had to learn all of the building codes for the city. I got copies of the codes and reviewed each one, making notes. If I did not understand something, I asked questions of expert staff members. I also visited construction sites to get a better understanding.

Behavioral interview question: Tell me about a course on government that you have taken.

Right answer: I took a course on government leadership offered by Genoa College. This course included tours of several state capitals and meetings with legislators, who explained the procedures for policy setting and law making.

Situational interview question: If you won the mayoral race, what information would you want to know?

Right answer: I would try to learn everything that I could about city government in the first month of my term. I would visit every department, get and read copies of policies and procedures used by each department, and talk with local community leaders about the most important issues.

Situational interview question: If you took a course on funding sources, how would you prepare for each lesson?

Right answer: I would carefully read every assignment and complete each exercise. After each exam, I would review the material to make sure that I understood every item that I missed.

Influence Skills

See the questions from scenario 4 and use wording that fits city governance.

Visionary

Behavioral interview question: In your current job, what do you see in the future for the department?

Right answer: In my mind, I see a very positive future. I see organized construction sites, fewer accidents, and better-quality buildings going up in the city.

Behavioral interview question: Think of a time when another person tried to sabotage something that you were trying to accomplish. How did you deal with that?

Right answer: I was trying to implement a streamlined record-keeping system. I talked with the individual and we found out that she had discovered a problem that I had not anticipated. Once that was resolved, she was on board. (Note that what you are listening for is some statement or indication that when the candidate sets a goal, he or she is driven to achieve it.)

Situational interview question: If you are elected, what do you see in the future of this city? How will you achieve it?

Right answer: I envision growth in jobs, industry, and property values. I see better-educated students. I plan to work through various community groups and businesspeople to find the keys to growth and then find the funding necessary to implement the plans.

Situational interview question: If you find that there is something inherently wrong with this community that has inhibited its growth, how will you approach the problem?

Right answer: Cities in arid deserts, areas with bitter winters, and dense forests have been able to grow and thrive in this country. There is no reason that a city like ours with good water resources, well-educated people, and room for expansion cannot do so as well. We must sell our strengths and find ways to overcome the real concerns.

Interpersonal Skills

See the questions from scenario 3 and use wording that fits city governance.

Persistence

Behavioral interview question: Think of a time when you encountered a big problem while working on a project. Describe it and tell me how you dealt with it.

Right answer: Our budget was cut in the middle of the record-keeping system update. After selecting the right software, we found that we could not afford it. I worked with other divisions that would benefit from an expedited system, and we pieced together the funding.

Behavioral interview question: Talk about a program you oversaw that moved along too slowly. How did you handle it?

Right answer: I was disappointed that our new park development program moved so slowly. I had to rein in my enthusiasm and work through the process. This requires patience, but it was worth it.

Situational interview question: If you were told that a potential business opportunity for the city was no longer available, what would you do?

Right answer: I would ask again after finding out why the deal fell through.

Situational interview question: If you were unable to hire the person you had identified as best for a particular position in city government, how would you handle it?

Right answer: I would research the reasons why the individual said no. I would find a solution to those concerns and ask again.

Ability to Deal with Frustration and Ambiguity

See the questions from scenario 4 and use wording that fits city governance.

Creativity

See the questions from scenario 4 and use wording that fits city governance.

Self-Confidence

Behavioral interview question: Describe a time when you had to take on a new challenge. How did you prepare?

Right answer: I knew nothing about parks when I was assigned that program. I read everything I could find on the subject and talked to everyone I knew with expertise. Then I jumped into the project and learned as I worked.

Behavioral interview question: Tell me about a situation where you had to get help from very successful people from outside your community. How did you interact with them?

Right answer: On the parks project, I attended a national seminar on parks and city government. Everyone there knew more than I did. My attitude was that I would learn as much as I could so that this would never be the case again.

Situational interview question: If you are faced with a situation where you do not know the answer, what will you do?

Right answer: I will do research and talk with experienced mayors from other cities to find out how others have handled this type of problem in the past. I will then make the decision that I think is best for our city.

Situational interview question: If you are thrown a curve ball by one of the city council members, what will you do?

Right answer: I will talk with that individual and find out what happened. I will do a bit more homework in the future to ensure fewer surprises.

Willingness to Travel and Meet with Corporate Decision Makers

Behavioral interview question: Tell me about a trip that you have taken to meet with a business leader.

Right answer: I flew to Seattle to meet with Bill Gates to help with our new broadband system. He invited a group of small city government leaders to identify our needs.

Situational interview question: Is there any reason that you would be unable to travel several times per month to a variety of locations around the country?

Right answer: No. (Note that this is a straightforward closed-ended question. If the candidate says yes, he or she would have to be eliminated from consideration if travel is part of the job.)

Scenario 6: CEO of a Large Urban Hospital

Respect for Tradition

Behavioral interview question: Describe a situation in your current job where there was a policy that you wanted to change. How did you do it?

Right answer: Despite hiring only nurses with bachelor's degrees, I found that we still had a nursing education program that cost $600,000 per year. This is an outdated concept in many hospitals, but one that is deeply rooted in hospital tradition. I began to make small changes in the program and found promotional opportunities for the nurses who were doing the training. Over a period of four years, we phased out the program, and I believe that everyone is more satisfied with our new approaches to training new nurses.

Behavioral interview question: What is the strongest tradition in the hospital in which you currently work? How does that affect your day-to-day work?

Right answer: Our hospital, like many others, was originally a religious organization. The attitude about how we treat people, especially the poor, has not changed, although we no longer have our religious affiliation. Our values regarding human kindness and service are things that are important to maintain.

Situational interview question: If a new medical director wanted to make many major changes that go against some hospital traditions, what would you do?

Right answer: I would assess the importance of the proposed changes. If they are changes that are critical to the health of the patients, I would work closely with those who guard traditions to help them see how the changes are consistent with the hospital's values. I would involve everyone in the change process.

Situational interview question: What do you consider to be your most important personal habit and how do you maintain it?

Right answer: I start every day with exercise. I believe that this helps both my mental and physical health, makes me a better husband and father, and prepares me for the long days that I work.

Consistent Values

See the questions from scenario 2 and use wording that fits a health care environment.

Positive Attitude Toward Patients and Health Care Professionals

See the questions from scenario 3 and use wording that fits a health care environment.

Initiative

See the questions from scenario 2 and use wording that fits a health care environment.

Visionary

See the questions from scenario 5 and use wording that fits a health care environment.

Considerate

See the questions from scenario 3 and use wording that fits a health care environment.

Interpersonal Skills

See the questions from scenario 3 and use wording that fits a health care environment.

Creativity

See the questions from scenario 4 and use wording that fits a health care environment.

Scenario 7: Your Position

Now try to create interview questions for the leadership position important to you. First, list four of the attributes you have identified that would be best measured by a structured interview. Then write two behavioral and two situational interview questions for each. Do not forget to include the right answers.

Position title: _____

Attribute 1: _____

Behavioral interview question: _____

_____

Right answer: _____

_____

Behavioral interview question: _____

_____

Right answer: _____

_____

Situational interview question: _____

_____

Right answer: _____

_____

Situational interview question: _____

_____

Right answer: ————————————————————————

—————————————————————————————————————

Attribute 2: ————————————————————

Behavioral interview question: ——————————————

—————————————————————————————————————

Right answer: ————————————————————————

—————————————————————————————————————

Behavioral interview question: ——————————————

—————————————————————————————————————

Right answer: ————————————————————————

—————————————————————————————————————

Situational interview question: ——————————————

—————————————————————————————————————

Right answer: ————————————————————————

—————————————————————————————————————

Situational interview question: ——————————————

—————————————————————————————————————

Right answer: ————————————————————————

—————————————————————————————————————

Attribute 3: ————————————————————

Behavioral interview question: ——————————————

—————————————————————————————————————

Right answer: ————————————————————————

—————————————————————————————————————

Behavioral interview question: _____

_____

Right answer: _____

_____

Situational interview question: _____

_____

Right answer: _____

_____

Situational interview question: _____

_____

Right answer: _____

_____

Attribute 4: _____

Behavioral interview question: _____

_____

Right answer: _____

_____

Behavioral interview question: _____

_____

Right answer: _____

_____

Situational interview question: _____

_____

Right answer: _____

_____

Situational interview question: _____

_____

    Right answer: _____

_____

Putting the Pieces Together

Now that you have gathered the data, it is time to decide which person to select for the leadership position. There are several steps that you can take to help you sort through the information. You must prioritize (or weight) the attributes that you identified if you have not already done so, rate the candidates on the attributes measured with tests or work samples, and compare ratings and notes with everyone who interviewed the candidates. I will walk you through each step.

Assigning Weights to Each Attribute

The first thing that must be done is to go back to the weights that you assigned to each attribute. This was discussed in chapter 7. The weights should be determined prior to the interview. The reason for this is that sometimes a candidate who is influential (maybe due to qualifications, appearance, or connections) may sway your ideas about what is important for the job. For example, as you consider which candidate your party should support for mayor, you could meet a candidate with very strong speaking skills. The speaking skills may create a halo effect that makes speaking skills look more important than vision. You change the weights (maybe on paper, or maybe just in your head) and select the individual with strong speaking skills. Your party's candidate is elected, and the city is stuck with a person who talks a good game but cannot lead. Make decisions about weights carefully and then stick with them.

Using the six scenarios, here are examples of how the weights or points may have been distributed for all of the attributes identified in chapter 3. Some of the weights for the attributes have a brief explanation provided if the value is not obvious. You may disagree with the values assigned in the examples. If so, how would you change the point distribution and why?

Scenario 1: President of Sunshine Fishing Club

Honesty: 15 points. Especially important because the president will be handling others' money.

Conscientiousness: 10 points.

Optimism: 5 points.

Friendliness: 10 points. Important for a club president.

An interest in other people: 5 points.

Emotional stability: 5 points.

Likes fishing: 5 points.

Good fishing skills: 5 points.

Planning and organizing skills: 20 points. This is the most important aspect of the leadership position.

Handling large sums of money well: 10 points. This is critical when handling other people's money.

Understanding of or willingness to learn the travel business: 5 points. This can be learned.

Minimal leadership experience: 5 points. This is a small club and past experience is not critical.

Scenario 2: Vice President of Planning for a Fortune 500 Company

Intelligence: 5 points. Intelligence, like all of the other attributes, is important. For this leadership position, most of the attributes carry equal weight.

Conscientiousness: 10 points.

Extroversion: 5 points.

Optimism: 5 points.

Energy level: 5 points.

Future oriented: 7 points. A leader involved in strategic planning must have a strong future orientation.

Self-confidence: 5 points.

Persistence: 8 points. Developing and executing a strategic plan is very difficult and can be frustrating. The leader must be persistent.

Computer skills: 5 points.

Organizational skills: 5 points.

Writing skills: 5 points.

Business knowledge: 10 points. To develop a workable plan, the leader must have a strong grounding in every aspect of business.

Knowledge of the industry and the law: 5 points.

Consistent values: 5 points.

Positive attitude toward all aspects of business: 5 points.

Initiative: 5 points.

Participative style of leadership: 5 points.

Scenario 3: High School Principal

Conscientiousness: 10 points. Conscientiousness is critical to this type of leader.

Extroversion: 3 points. All of the attributes are important and most will have equal weight.

Optimism: 3 points.

Energy level: 3 points.

Emotional stability: 15 points. Due to the difficult nature of this job and the continuous interaction with children, teachers, and parents, sometimes in very stressful situations, emotional stability is essential.

Present oriented: 3 points.

Persistence: 3 points.

Self-confidence: 3 points.

Honesty: 3 points.

Saltiness: 3 points.

Leadership experience: 3 points.

Family oriented: 3 points.

Consistent values: 3 points.

Positive attitude toward children: 10 points. This leader must like children and enjoy working with them.

Detail oriented: 3 points.

Willing to constantly monitor performance data: 3 points.

Considerate toward teachers and staff: 3 points.

Interpersonal skills: 3 points.

Knowledge of education, teaching, and administration: 20 points. This position requires a very strong understanding of the basics of education.

Scenario 4: Director of Public Relations for a Historical Society

Conscientiousness: 3 points. Most of the attributes are equally important.

Extroversion: 3 points.

Friendliness: 3 points.

Cooperativeness: 3 points.

Optimism: 3 points.

High energy level: 3 points.

Future oriented: 3 points.

Self-confidence: 3 points.

Excellent writing skills: 15 points. Since this leader will write press releases and work on all pamphlets and educational materials produced by the society, strong writing skills are necessary.

Knowledge of the media and public relations: 4 points.

Basic knowledge of or willingness to learn about the historical society: 3 points. Note that this can be easily and quickly learned.

Strong knowledge of marketing, advertising, and promotion: 10 points. This leader must have a thorough understanding of and experience in each aspect of public relations.

Consistent values: 3 points.

Positive attitude about the value of the work of the society: 3 points.

Ability to deal with frustration and ambiguity: 3 points.

Interpersonal skills: 20 points. This leader will interact on a continuous basis with community officials, potential donors, and the media.

Influence skills: 3 points.

Creativity: 12 points. This position will require a high level of creativity.

Scenario 5: Mayor of a Midsized City in the Rust Belt

Friendliness: 3 points. This attribute's importance is equal to that of most other attributes required for this position.

Cooperativeness: 3 points.

Optimism: 3 points.

Speaking skills: 10 points. Being able to connect with the voters is essential to getting elected.

High energy level: 3 points.

Organizational skills: 3 points.

Understanding of or willingness to learn about local laws and government at all levels: 25 points. Making sure that local laws are followed is critical for this leader.

Influence skills: 12 points. The mayor must influence others to work hard for the benefit of the community.

Visionary: 20 points. If the community requires growth into the future, a visionary leader is necessary.

Interpersonal skills: 3 points.

Persistence: 3 points.

Ability to deal with frustration and ambiguity: 3 points.

Creativity: 3 points.

Self-confidence: 3 points.

Willingness to travel and meet with corporate decision makers: 3 points.

Scenario 6: CEO of a Large Urban Hospital

Intelligence: 3 points. Most of the attributes for this position carry equal weight.

Conscientiousness: 3 points.

Extroversion: 3 points.

Future oriented: 3 points.

Friendly: 3 points.

Cooperativeness: 3 points.

Optimism: 3 points.

Energy level: 3 points.

Persistence: 3 points.

Self-confidence: 3 points.

Emotional stability: 3 points.

Honesty: 3 points.

Organizational skills: 3 points.

Understanding of hospital administration and health care: 10 points. This is clearly the primary attribute for this leader.

Knowledge of the law in the field: 3 points. The hospital attorney can advise the CEO on the details of these matters.

Influence skills: 10 points. A hospital CEO must spend a great deal of time influencing others both within and outside the organization.

Respect for tradition: 3 points.

Consistent values: 3 points.

Positive attitude with patients and health care professionals: 10 points. A positive attitude is essential to achieving the hospital's goals.

Initiative: 3 points.

Visionary: 3 points.

Considerate: 3 points.

Strong interpersonal skills: 10 points. The CEO must interact well with many constituents.

Creativity: 3 points.

Scenario 7: Your Position

Now, you try it with the leadership position important to you.

Position title: _____

Attributes   Weights

_____   _____
_____   _____
_____   _____
_____   _____
_____   _____
_____   _____
_____   _____
_____   _____
_____   _____
_____   _____
_____   _____
_____   _____

Rating the Candidates

The second step is to rate each candidate on each of the attributes. If you used an interview to measure attributes, you should already have

rated the candidate on those attributes. Using a three-point rating system, rate the candidates on each of the attributes measured with either a
personality test or a work sample. The system that I recommended earlier
was this:

0. The candidate does not have the required attribute.
1. The candidate has the required attribute.
2. The candidate is superior in terms of the required attribute.

With personality and cognitive ability tests, you should establish a
minimally acceptable score. This score represents the level necessary to
successfully fulfill the job responsibilities. You can determine that score
by giving the test to other successful job holders and by consulting with
experts. Every candidate who scores at or above that minimal score
would be given a rating of 1. If you used an expert to conduct the
personality testing, have that person help you establish the minimum
score. Candidates who score considerably above the minimum score
would be rated 2. What score would earn a rating of 2 should be established ahead of time.

This idea of establishing a minimum score may sound a bit strange
because it is tempting to simply rank order the candidates by their scores.
In some cases, this may be a good strategy. The reason that establishing a
minimum is more effective is because most of us have good and bad days
when we take tests. On Monday, we might score 155 on conscientiousness whereas on Thursday we would score 160. Although the scores
are close enough to be considered statistically reliable (i.e., there is not
really any difference in the two scores so it does not matter), a ranking
strategy would place a candidate with a score of 160 above another with
a score of 155. Unless you have evidence that a higher score will really
make a difference in performance, obtaining a minimum score is all that
really matters.

Scores on work samples represent actual work that the leader might be
doing and will provide a consistent and valid predictor of job performance. Assign a rating based on the quality of the work sample. It is best,
but not always feasible, to obtain the work sample as part of your testing
and interviewing process. For example, after the interviews are done,
give the candidates for director of public relations an assignment to test
creativity. Ask them to create a design for a brochure for a new exhibit

on Native Americans in southwestern Ohio. Give them about thirty to sixty minutes to rough out an idea.

Be careful, however, of examples of past work performance. When examples of past work are presented, you may not have proof that the candidate actually did the work. For example, you may ask a candidate for director of public relations for a work sample and receive a well-designed professional brochure. Be sure that the candidate is the one who designed and wrote the piece if those attributes matter to you. A brochure done by an ad agency or a candidate's subordinate will not tell you that the candidate can design and write.

It is now time to compare the candidates. Calculate a score for each attribute by multiplying the weight by the rating. You can use a spreadsheet to line up the candidates on each attribute and calculate an overall score for each. As an example, let's take the leadership position for the fourth scenario. A spreadsheet for this position might look like table 8.1.

In this example, candidate 3 has the highest score according to your ratings. Since candidate 2's score is close, you will want to carefully review your information about that individual to ensure fairness. It appears that candidate 1 is out.

Comparing Your Ratings

Step 3 in this process is to compare your ratings with those of other interviewers. If you find that your ratings are either significantly above or below those of other interviewers, you should have a long conversation about how you each developed your ratings. The advantage of a panel interview is that you have all heard and seen the responses to the same questions. Sometimes different people interpret responses differently. This is the time to compare what you have heard with others. Either you or the other interviewers may change their ratings after the discussion.

With any luck, you will all have similar ratings and will arrive at the same decision on which candidate to hire. If not, there are a couple of strategies you can use. First, you can simply add all of the scores together and hire the one with the highest combined score. Second, if one of you feels strongly about a candidate whom other interviewers did not like, you can discuss it further. If the interviewer who differs can point out

Table 8.1 Sample Comparison of Ratings for Candidates for Director of Public Relations for a Historical Society

Attribute	Weight	Rating/Score for Three Candidates (Rating × Weight)		
		1	2	3
Conscientiousness	3	1/3	1/3	1/3
Extroversion	3	0/0	1/3	1/3
Friendliness	3	0/0	1/3	1/3
Cooperativeness	3	1/3	1/3	1/3
Optimism	3	0/0	1/3	2/6
High energy level	3	1/3	1/3	2/6
Future oriented	3	0/0	1/3	2/6
Self-confidence	3	1/3	1/3	1/3
Excellent writing skills	15	1/15	2/30	1/15
Knowledge of media and public relations	4	2/8	2/8	2/8
Basic knowledge of historical society	3	1/3	1/3	1/3
Strong knowledge of marketing, advertising, and promotion	10	1/10	1/10	2/20
Consistent values	3	1/3	1/3	2/6
Positive attitude about the value of the work of the society	3	1/3	0/0	1/3
Ability to deal with frustration and ambiguity	3	2/6	0/0	1/3
Interpersonal skills	20	0/0	1/20	1/20
Influence skills	3	0/0	1/3	0/6
Creativity	12	1/12	1/12	1/12
Total score for each candidate		72	113	123

information that the rest of you missed, you may want to reconsider your ratings. However, if the interviewer is going strictly on a gut feeling, you would be better served to stick to your original assessment.

Be very careful about ignoring low ratings and hiring a candidate with high curb appeal. Often, that type of appeal is based on physical and demographic characteristics. When you allow non-work-related information to enter your selection decision, it often results in selecting a poor leader for your organization. It could also lead to an accusation of discrimination. With a structured system like the one presented in this book, you should hire more effective leaders. In addition, you will have evidence that you really worked at filling the position (which matters to your boss and your constituents) and did not discriminate (which matters to the legal system).

What if you and the other interviewers and testers rate two candidates the same? It can happen, and it is more likely if you have done a good job of recruiting candidates. Go back to the questions in the previous chapter.

Which leader candidate complements the staff that you currently have? To answer this question, you must do an assessment of your current staff. What skills and abilities are missing and which candidate can fill the gaps?

Does one candidate have a special skill, expertise, or characteristic (for example, a second language) that would add value to the organization? If you are planning to open an office in Brazil and one of the candidates speaks Portuguese, that could give you an advantage.

Did one of the candidates offend you or others during the selection process? Did one of the candidates make a sexist comment or joke that offended someone? Did one of the candidates act abrasive or confrontational when talking about a former employer?

Did one of the candidates make you and others feel particularly comfortable during the interview? Was there one candidate who had very strong presence? Did someone interact particularly well with the interview panel?

Are you sure that your comfort level with a candidate is not based on gender, race, ethnicity, religion, former college, neighborhood where the candidate grew up, or something else? Unless you are hiring someone for a leadership position with a BFOQ, you should not take any non-job-related factors into consideration. One example of a BFOQ would be that the applicants for a priest position in a Catholic church must be male. As long as it is church policy that women cannot be priests, you may legally discriminate against female applicants for this job.

Making an Offer

Once the new leader is chosen, you should offer the position either in person or over the telephone. Tell the individual why you chose him or her. If this is a paid leadership role, the compensation (which includes benefits) should be discussed. This is your last opportunity to promote your organization. Use it!

I recommend that the dollar amount that will be offered to a candidate not be discussed until this stage. The reason is that you will not know until you complete your screening process how much a candidate is worth. If you find a gem, you can often find more money, even in the public sector. Talking about money early on can be misleading or focus attention on the money rather than the other opportunities that the position offers. It is OK to provide a salary range as a point of information earlier in the process, but not a specific salary that will be offered. With leadership positions (except those that do not pay at all), it should be assumed that the position will pay what the market requires. If your organization pays less than market value for a leadership position, this would be something to share earlier as well. If so, good luck hiring qualified leaders! If you are unsure about the market value of a particular leadership position, talk to a compensation specialist to get this information.

Again, keep in mind that different people are worth different salaries depending on their experience and skill level. With most leadership positions at senior levels, some negotiation will be involved in determining the final offer. You should know, before you begin to recruit, the maximum salary that you can afford to pay, considering the required qualifications.

Depending on the level of the position, you may get an immediate response or the candidate may ask for time to consider the offer. To head off being asked for long periods of time to consider an offer, you can state during the interview process that you will make a decision by a set date and will expect an answer within a specific period of time. Simply say, "We will make a decision by March 15. The person we choose will be called on that day. We will need an answer by Friday morning. Would that be a problem for you?" Then stick with it.

It is not uncommon for someone who is on the job market to be pursuing several opportunities at the same time and to want to delay accepting one offer to see if another organization will offer more. I recently observed a situation where an offer was made and the person chosen stalled for two full weeks, only to turn down the job for another with a competitor. Of course, our offer was used to negotiate a higher salary with the other organization.

This situation caused three problems. One, it wasted our time. Two, it suggested that the candidate did not want to be a leader in our organization. Either we had not done a good job recruiting or we had not done a good job promoting our organization. Three, other candidates were left hanging. The one we hired knew that he was not our first choice.

Generally, when the position is volunteer work, like the president of a social club or a civic group, it will involve a lot of work and very little reward. When the offer is made, you must highlight the benefits of the position. Every leadership position has some advantage to the leader.

As soon as your choice for the position accepts, mail kind rejection letters to the other candidates. These letters should highlight how much you enjoyed meeting the person, his or her skills and abilities, what the chosen candidate had that the others did not, and how much you appreciate the individual applying for the position and going through the process. For example, you may say, "We enjoyed meeting you and hope that we will see you at future conferences. You have excellent engineering skills. The person we chose had language skills that will be helpful when we open our office in Brazil. We appreciate the time and energy that you put into the selection process." Many organizations make the mistake of not notifying the people who are not selected. Inevitably, you will deal with each of these candidates again in some capacity, either directly or indirectly. They should not have been finalists for your position without having good qualifications. Do not leave them with the feeling that they were used or rejected. It will come back at you in some form if you do.

Developing Leaders to Fit the Organization

Since you have hired the best candidate to lead, he or she is bound to be successful. Correct? Unfortunately, that is not correct. It rarely works that way. One of the biggest mistakes that you can make is assuming that if someone has the credentials to lead, he or she will lead your organization in the manner and direction you desire.

Strangely enough, leaders who are effective in one organization often fail miserably in other positions. We frequently see that with CEOs of Fortune 500 companies. Even when a leader moves to an organization in the same industry, organizational culture, including the management philosophy and values of the stakeholders, can affect CEO performance. Unless the leader chosen is an internal candidate, it is the responsibility of supervisors and others to make sure that the new leader has a clear understanding of the organization's business and mission, the goals of the stakeholders, the staff members, the management philosophy, the CEO's vision, and the history of the organization. How is this accomplished?

The Mission and Business of the Organization

Many good candidates will ask about the mission, vision, and goals of the organization during the selection process. Probably the best way to communicate this type of information is through a personal meeting. Depending on the type of organization, the meeting should be held with the CEO and other senior-level executives in a business setting, the city council in city government, the board of a nonprofit organization, or the membership of a social club. It is essential that a leader knows the primary reason for the organization's existence, the future direction, and the interim goals of the organization in order to lead effectively. Ideally, this information would have been communicated during the selection process to provide ample opportunity for the candidates to make sure that there is a good fit with their skills, interests, and personal goals.

The business of an organization refers to the types of products or services that it sells or provides to customers or clients. The business of an organization may be coordinating activities for a group with similar interests, public education, or selling ball bearings. The mission of an organization refers to the primary and specific reason that it exists. Is it supposed to make money? Is it supposed to educate children from kindergarten through sixth grade? Is it serving underprivileged minorities? Is it trying to build a better county government? Is it promoting the value of preserving historical sites in the state? Typically, the business and mission of an organization can be summarized in one or two sentences. It would be safe to assume that a recently hired leader understands the business and mission of your organization. However, if the mission is a bit more obscure, you may need to communicate it more clearly. For example, years ago, a CEO of an international airline realized that his company was not in the transportation industry but rather the service industry. The new focus on service became the driving force in turning around a business that had not been doing well. To be successful, this message had to be communicated to everyone in the organization. Disney's mission is entertainment and in their orientation sessions, all new hires are referred to as cast members. In these examples, the mission drives the culture. A good explanation is, therefore, critical to understanding a leadership role.

Goals of the Stakeholders

The goals of the stakeholders are more complex. The manager or board of the organization should give the newly hired leader a detailed explanation of what each constituent wants to achieve. Then the new leader should visit with representatives of each of the stakeholders. With the president of a social club, this will simply be an open discussion about the future of the club at the next meeting. However, the new CEO of a hospital will have a much more difficult task of understanding complicated and sometimes diverse goals of different constituents. Let's look at this challenge more closely.

A hospital has many stakeholders. Each group of stakeholders will have unique goals. Here is a list of each group, the best way to understand their point of view, and potential goals of each.

1. *The hospital board.* A board meeting should be held and the CEO should meet with each board member individually. Their goals:

   - Ensure the efficient operation of the hospital
   - Provide service to the community
   - Raise money for a new cardiac care center
   - Avoid controversy and problems
   - Ensure the integrity of the hospital

2. *The medical staff.* A meeting of the medical staff should be held and the CEO should meet with the medical director of the hospital and directors of each medical unit. Their goals:

   - Obtain the best medical technology and equipment
   - Work with the best professional staff possible (i.e., interns, nurses, pharmacists, medical technologists, etc.)
   - Create and sustain a healthy work environment
   - Control infectious disease in the community
   - Serve the community
   - Maximize earnings

3. *Employees.* The new CEO should visit departmental meetings and invite employees to the CEO's office via an open-door policy, meetings with union or professional representatives of organizations, and informal conversations in the hallways and cafeteria. Employees' goals:

   - Serve the community
   - Achieve or maintain good working conditions

- Obtain the best technology and equipment
- Work with the best physicians possible
- Get ahead in their specialized fields
- Maximize earnings

4. *Local political leaders.* The new CEO should attend community meetings that political leaders attend, and request private meetings to discuss their ideas, suggestions, and concerns about the hospital. Their goals:

- Serve the community
- Improve the public perception of the community's hospitals
- Ensure that the community has top-quality medical care
- Influence hospital decisions that affect the level of medical care available in the community
- Attract new businesses to the community by impressing them with the quality of medical care available

5. *Major donors.* The new CEO should schedule private meetings with all of the largest contributors to the hospital, and attend all events held by the development staff. Their goals:

- Serve the community
- Ensure that their contributions are used appropriately
- Ensure that proper recognition is given for gifts, particularly those given to honor or memorialize a loved one
- Meet the medical needs of the community
- Find ways to reduce their taxes as they relate to charitable contributions

6. *Patients and their families.* The new CEO should have informal discussions with patients and families during hospital stays, and should review all patient satisfaction survey data. Their goals:

- Get well
- Obtain the best medical care available in the world
- Reduce out-of-pocket costs for patients

- Have a pleasant, comfortable, safe, and risk-free environment in the hospital

Current Staff

The next part of the orientation of the new leader is a thorough introduction to the current staff including executives and other professionals. It seems counterintuitive, but many leaders do not make meeting other members of the organization a priority. They forget that leaders get work done through others. The very nature of leadership necessitates knowing the staff well. However, there is an explanation for this phenomenon. Many successful leaders feel in control and they are typically motivated by a need to be in control. Effective leaders have learned that the quality of their work is affected by the quality of the work of their followers.

A large hospital might have thousands of employees, so the CEO is unlikely to have the need, time, or desire to meet every employee. However, the CEO must know the entire executive team, including the administrative assistants, all managers at the director level and above, and everyone handling public relations and development— within the first month. As time goes on, the CEO will meet many other members of the staff.

Meeting such a large group of people takes a great deal of time. It also requires multiple meetings of different types. A reception honoring the new CEO may be one of the first meetings with the staff. The less formal this initial meeting, the better. Regardless of the level of formality, the CEO should make some remarks about the direction in which the hospital will be heading. These informal large group meetings should be followed with private lunches with key staff members after a review of the resumes of each.

Although rarely done, a CEO can ask each staff member to send a tailored resume with personal information and a photo. A tailored resume would summarize the key aspects of the person's education and experience relevant to his or her current job. For example, the CEO may not need to know that a staff member took specific undergraduate courses typically listed on a resume. The leader does need to know how long the staff member has been the director of security and what recent training she has completed on safety. These resumes could be sent prior to the CEO's start date and will give the new leader a head start on learning names and developing a better understanding of the hospital staff.

In the case of a CEO, the head of the board or an executive vice president can request the resumes and organize the meetings. When a lower-level leader has been selected, the CEO should take the lead on making sure the appropriate meetings are scheduled.

At the opposite end of the spectrum, the director of public relations for a public agency will have to request meetings with all of the people who will supervise his work as well as those whose work he will direct. The president of a social club will have less work to do if she has been active in the club. Assuming active membership for at least a year, she probably has a good knowledge of the capabilities and interests of the club members. The new principal of a school hired from the outside will need to work very hard to meet every teacher and establish a good rapport. This can be done with an informal picnic on the first day that teachers report along with individual visits to classrooms while teachers are setting up their rooms. Helping teachers carry books and supplies or put up bulletin boards would provide an opportunity to interact.

Any meeting where a new leader provides assistance to followers and works side by side with them will be the most valuable setting. Since newly hired or promoted managers are frequently overwhelmed with their own tasks, working with staff members means that the leader will have to work late hours for a few weeks. It is an investment that will pay off tenfold. In some very progressive organizations, CEOs work on the factory floor on occasion throughout their tenure. It is a great way to understand the work and the workers.

Management Philosophy

The management philosophy of an organization is typically something that evolves over time and is an integral part of the culture. Given that history, the management philosophy is often difficult to change. New leaders need to understand the philosophy even if they do not like that style, for a couple of obvious reasons.

One, new leaders will be managed using the organization's management philosophy. They will be better able to anticipate how their superiors will behave and what they will expect if they thoroughly understand the philosophy.

Two, a new leader will manage others who are used to being treated in a certain fashion. If the previous boss was authoritarian, followers may lack initiative or be overly dependent on the leader for direction. A leader may see that behavior as inadequacy, when followers are actually responding to the environment. If the organization uses a participative style, followers may resent a new leader who makes all of the decisions.

Three, there may be an expectation that the new leader will adapt to the management philosophy or that the leader will change the philosophy. Either way, the leader has to understand where people are coming from at the outset.

Understanding an organization's management philosophy is not a simple thing to do. Probably, good leaders have already asked about that during the interview process. In many organizations, managers will tell you that their company believes in participative management, encourages creativity, empowers workers, and believes in horizontal communication. Few actually do, however. Most managers follow a strict chain of command and believe that maintaining control is essential. Helping a new leader find out how management is practiced in a large company is difficult. The following are some approaches:

1. Arrange meetings for the leader with workers in the department or team and ask them to share critical incidents—situations that occurred which are out of the ordinary. Ask them to talk about how managers responded to the situation. Find out what happened to those managers. For example, if a manager fired a person who made a mistake and the manager is now a vice president, that tells the new leader what is valued about management. If, on the other hand, a manager implemented a training program for the person who made the mistake and the manager was promoted, the leader will get a different message about the philosophy.
2. Arrange a meeting for the leader with senior executives and ask them to talk about the best managers they have had. The leader will learn what type of management behavior is valued.
3. Give the new leader some specific examples of events that have occurred in this department, how the previous leader managed the situation, and why the leader was successful or not.

It is important to note that an organization's management philosophy is not open for debate, unless they are doing something illegal or immoral like torturing people or firing them without reason. Some management teams prefer authoritarian styles of management and others prefer participative styles. Both styles can work, particularly when they are practiced consistently. Management philosophies can also change or evolve over time. New CEOs may be able to influence the philosophy more than lower-level leaders. It may be possible for lower-level leaders to use a style that works well for them even when it conflicts with the organizational management philosophy. However, this may not work in all situations, especially if one is trying to use an authoritarian style in a participative organization. Given this, it is best to talk about management philosophy during the interview and then provide a comprehensive explanation during the orientation.

Organizational Vision

A leader's vision is the cognitive image of what an organization can become. The more detailed it is, the more likely the organization is to achieve that vision and the more direction lower-level leaders will have. Newly selected leaders must know what the vision is and how their department fits into the overall picture.

The CEO's vision should be communicated during the first week or two by the CEO. The most important piece of the vision is the part that applies to the new leader. Every member of the organization should have a general understanding of what the CEO hopes to accomplish. But the new principal of the high school should know very specifically if the superintendent of the district wants a 10 percent increase in standardized test scores, a 20 percent decline in classroom disciplinary problems, and 10 percent fewer dropouts in the coming year. The new CEO of the hospital should know that the board wants to improve patient satisfaction by 20 percent, reduce costs by 10 percent, and have a larger presence on civic committees. The director of public relations for the historical society must know that the president of the historical society wants increased press coverage of all of their openings and events.

It is also important that new leaders understand the history of the organization. It is very common for CEOs to be hired from outside an organization. The thinking is that the skills that make one an effective leader in one organization will transfer to the other. In general, this may be true. Nonetheless, the history of an organization influences the management philosophy and, in general, the way business is done. Several examples of mistakes spring to mind. When Apple hired John Sculley, he failed to understand the high-tech culture created by the founders. When he fired Jacques Nasser, Bill Ford commented that Nasser was not running Ford like the family-owned business that it was.

Can mistakes be avoided if a new CEO is better trained on the history and background of the organization? Perhaps. Note that we tend to prefer future-oriented CEOs who will spend very little time considering the past history of the organizations that they lead.[1] However, the founders, owners, long-term employees, and major stockholders still think about the company in terms of its past and have parallel expectations. This means that often we hire leaders whose temporal alignment is not conducive to understanding the history of an organization. If we select them, it is our job to make sure that they understand.

Skill Development

During the selection process, attributes were outlined and used to pick the best leader for the job. It would be highly unusual for the leader who was selected to have all of the desirable attributes. The candidate who met most of the criteria was probably the one picked. One of the advantages of having a systematic selection procedure for hiring is that we know exactly where the weaknesses are as well. We should never settle for the lesser of two evils when selecting leaders. We should hire the best qualified and then train the leader in the weak areas.

For example, refer back to table 8.1, where the attributes of three candidates are summarized. Candidate 3 would probably be the person who was hired. Note, however, that candidate 3 appears to be lacking in influence skills. This would be an area where training would be helpful. Perhaps a sales trainer in the organization could do the training. If not, send candidate 3 to a workshop, course, or seminar to develop this attribute. In a real situation, the candidate who is hired will probably need to participate in development activities in several areas.

For reasons that have to do primarily with ego, we often fail to develop people in leadership positions. How do you tell a CEO that he needs training? It is expected that once people have achieved leadership positions, they know everything or will pretend to at least. Many leaders will try to hide their deficiencies. In addition, the higher people are in an organization, the busier they tend to be. Finding time for training can be tough. Usually, because everyone works their way up the ladder, they do not have the experience and training necessary for the higher-level job. Train your leaders! They do a better job and last longer when you do.

There are a number of sources for leadership development. The following sections describe some, in no particular order.

Master of Business Administration Programs

The traditional MBA was geared toward people who earned their undergraduate degrees in humanities or engineering. Many of the new MBA programs are different. At Penn State Behrend, for example, the school offers advanced courses in business that would not have been taken by those who earned a bachelor's degree in business. New leaders should be encouraged to pursue their MBAs at the many evening, weekend, and online programs available around the country. Business leaders will get a broad perspective on the many different areas of their business, current management thinking and trends, and opportunities to practice business methods in a classroom (i.e., safe) environment. They can also improve their speaking, writing, negotiating, and interpersonal skills. It is common for business leaders to have degrees in fields other than business. For example, many executives in manufacturing companies have undergraduate degrees in engineering. They need to understand every aspect of business to be effective leaders.

Master's Programs in Specific Fields

There are master's degree programs in public administration, engineering management, health care management, school administration, nursing home administration, not-for-profit management, and so on. Finding a degree program specifically designed to develop leadership skills in a particular industry or field would be useful for leaders entering those organizations. For example, the individual selected to be the director of public relations for the historical society may have a degree in communications and experience working for a Fortune 500 company. She will need to understand public administration and how that differs from for-profit management.

Continuing Education Programs through Colleges and Universities

Many institutions of higher education offer noncredit courses in leadership and other specific areas of business. For example, a common course is Accounting for Nonaccountants. The subject areas range from dealing with difficult people to updates on new laws to how to negotiate. Every college that offers these courses will have a Web site that provides information or will mail information to interested people. Your organization should make a point of being on mailing lists and e-mail distribution lists for upcoming courses.

Training through Professional Organizations

In my opinion, professional organizations offer some of the better training programs. They tend to do the best job screening instructors, have very good professional designation preparation courses, and have a good handle on recent developments in the field. For example, the American Compensation Association offers excellent courses on compensation. Any leader with a college education in a professional field should belong to a professional organization and receive brochures on their upcoming training programs. These programs tend to be expensive but are well worth the cost.

For-Profit Training Companies

A number of for-profit organizations offer seminars and workshops for leaders. Be careful about quality and price, which are difficult to assess as the programs come and go. Consulting groups often spring up after popular leadership books are published. For example, after the publication and success of *The Seven Habits of Highly Effective People*, the consulting group of the author of that book did extensive training for leadership development in many companies. If you like the ideas in a particular book and want to disseminate them, such seminars may be a good idea. Keep in mind that the concepts found in popular business literature may not have been empirically tested or have much long-term impact.

One of the best-known leadership development organizations is the Center for Creative Leadership, with several locations around the country. They offer a variety of training programs and use extensive assessment to evaluate strengths and weaknesses of trainees. Their courses are well grounded in recent research, which they conduct, and the leadership literature.

Mentoring

One of the most effective methods of training leaders is through mentoring. Although we might hesitate to appoint a mentor for a CEO, most leaders would benefit from mentoring by an established member of the organization. Mentoring provides informal advice on structure, politics, people information, and history that cannot be learned otherwise. Even CEOs can request that a long-term executive mentor them on the organization's politics.

In-House Training Programs

If the organization has a qualified in-house leadership trainer, this is often a very good option. In-house staff should have an excellent understanding of the management philosophy, the organizational vision, and the corporate culture. Other executives can participate in the leadership development courses to make sure that consistent information is provided about goals and direction. Good corporate trainers advise CEOs about gaps in understanding of a leader's vision. The concepts and ideology that drive the leadership training should be widely discussed. Specific content should be driven by the strategic focus of the organization. Sometimes CEOs are surprised by what is being taught—that should never happen. Often CEOs rubber-stamp leadership training topics and philosophies that they do not practice themselves—that should never happen.

It is essential that whatever approach to leadership training is used, the philosophy being advocated and the concepts being taught in the program should be understood. Nothing is worse than sending a leader or a group of leaders to a training program that will not be useful to the organization or that contradicts the basic management philosophy.

Fifteen years ago, a Fortune 500 company arranged for a large consulting company to conduct a company-tailored version of a nationally known leadership training program for their management team. A group of 100 leaders traveled across country to Washington, DC, for five days. The cost of the training and travel came to approximately $500,000. Immediately upon their return, one of the leaders was told, "Forget all that stuff you learned in the training and get back to work."

Newly selected leaders require a great deal of development to be effective. "Hit the ground running" is a nice phrase, but it hardly ever works when we hire from the outside. It is the responsibility of the people who select the new leader to make sure that the leader has the skills and knowledge necessary to be successful.

Retaining Effective Leaders

Of the thousands of books and articles written on leadership, it is difficult to find one that specifically addresses the retention of effective leaders. Yet that is one of the most important problems facing organizations. Companies with top-notch leaders are the envy of other businesses and groups. It is quite common for effective leaders to be recruited away by other organizations. It is also common for leaders to become disillusioned and leave. Sometimes money draws leaders away, but often there are other reasons why they leave. The fit issues addressed in earlier chapters are part of that process. In addition, new leaders must be given support for the changes that they try to implement, along with sufficient resources. There must also be an investment in the programs they lead.

The cost of an effective new leader goes well beyond salary and benefits. It also includes the costs of recruiting, selecting, and training, the costs of working without a leader in place while conducting the search, and the reputation of the organization, which is often damaged by turnover of leaders. This chapter introduces a variety of strategies that can ensure that good leaders stay with an organization.

Note that I am talking about strong and effective leaders here. I am not talking about managers who may do their jobs and follow instructions well every day. We need good managers too, but they are relatively easy to find. Strong, effective leaders are not. We must retain these kinds of leaders for our organizations to be successful in the long term.

By *strong, effective leaders*, I am referring to people whom you would see doing the following:

1. They are proactive and take the initiative on assignments as well as initiating projects.
2. They think about the best alternatives for the organization, not just their department, their workers, or themselves.
3. They think about the future of the department, their projects, and the organization.
4. They pursue development and educational opportunities aggressively, paying for courses themselves if training is not provided by the company.
5. They are actively involved in the community.
6. They voluntarily participate in extra tasks that are not part of their job descriptions, like the United Way campaign and ad hoc committees.
7. They give opinions when asked and do not parrot their bosses. They are not afraid to talk to executives.
8. They take chances and try new things.
9. They are confident that they can do assigned tasks.
10. They are positive about the organization and the future.
11. They came to the organization motivated and do not rely on their bosses to motivate them.
12. Coworkers view them as leaders, look to them during discussions, count on their opinions, and go to them for help.
13. They enjoy playing a leadership role.
14. They are ambitious and want to hold higher-level positions.

Why Good Leaders Leave

Let's begin with a review of the many reasons that effective leaders leave organizations. Some are obvious and others are more complex. Keep in mind that there is hardly ever just one reason for a leader to resign. It is most likely that there is a combination of reasons.

Money

One of the strongest arguments for high CEO pay is that companies must pay exorbitant salaries, bonuses, and perks to retain their CEOs. This argument is made even when companies are losing money. The belief behind this naive theory is that very few people are capable of running a Fortune 100 or Fortune 500 company. Is it true that very few people are qualified to be a CEO? The general population of the country is not qualified, but there are thousands of men and women who could success-fully manage a Fortune 500 company. Is it true that CEOs are motivated to perform because of the millions that they are paid? Some are, but few CEOs make millions and research suggests that most CEOs are attracted to the power. This suggests that they would do the job for significantly less than they are paid. Will they jump to another company for a few million more? Maybe, but it is unlikely. Why? Because there are not many Fortune 500 and other large-company CEO positions available. Most of those are un-available most of the time. In addition, boards typically prefer inside candidates for CEO positions. Thus, while jumping from firm to firm happens, the risk is not as high as some CEO salaries suggest.

Other leaders at low levels in our organizations are much more vul-nerable to better salary offers from other firms. The reasons are simple. Usually, candidates for leadership positions are hoping to move up from a pay standpoint. In most organizations, we tend to worry less about losing lower-level leaders than we do CEOs, but the opposite should be our concern. The cost of keeping lower-level leaders is far less than the cost of hanging on to a CEO who is offered a million-dollar raise. The talented lower-level leaders in our organizations are the future. Ambitious young people who leave because they want and need to in-crease their earnings are both a present and future loss to us. The other reason is that more positions are available at lower levels. Someone who is willing to relocate to a new company has many options. Again, however, money is only part of the equation. The opportunity to move up is probably more or equally important to leaders at lower levels.

Advancement and Achievement

Many leaders leave their current employers when they have an oppor-tunity for a more challenging, complex, difficult, interesting, or satisfying position and when they do not see these opportunities with their current employer. On rare occasions, leaders will even take less money for a better job. They consider it an investment in their careers. Typically, strong, effective leaders are bright and often they are future oriented. These types of people are more apt to become bored with their current jobs.

Problems with the Current Position

The types of problems that motivate leaders to leave their jobs include the following:

- *Poor leadership.* strong leaders have less tolerance for poor leadership than other employees. They are the type of people who believe that they can do it better—although sometimes they are right and sometimes they are not.
- *Poor coworkers or followers.* Leaders care about the ability of their colleagues. When they are forced to work with people who are incapable, they may become frustrated.
- *Lack of control.* If leaders find themselves in situations where they cannot hire new employees or test their ideas, they become frustrated. If they have leadership roles where they have lots of responsibility but no ability to control the process, they will leave.
- *Insufficient resources.* If they do not have sufficient resources or staff to do their jobs, they will leave.
- *Poor working conditions.* If a work environment is uncomfortable or unpleasant, people will eventually leave.
- *Low morale at the current organization.* I am convinced that people will stay with an organization with great morale regardless of pay and promotional opportunities. If there is a strong sense of teamwork, an attitude that "we're in this together," and cohesiveness, many leaders will pass up opportunities at other organizations. Managers who rely on pay to keep good workers and managers are misguided, at best, and fools, at worst. Even ambitious people will wait for promotional opportunities in the right organization.

Unmet Needs

If a leader enjoys a changing environment but is stuck at a desk in an organization where there is little business travel or interaction with outside organizations, he will be likely to leave. If a leader enjoys diversity but is stuck in a department made up entirely of middle-aged white women, she will be more likely to leave. If a leader enjoys variety in her work assignments, but is stuck in a position where the tasks never vary, she will be more likely to leave. The list goes on and on.

Lack of Fit

Probably the most common and least talked about reason for leaving an organization is a lack of fit. This means that the leader is different in some way:

- *Values.* Perhaps the leader has been asked to do something that violates his or her personal ethics.
- *Attitudes about the balance between work and personal life.* Perhaps a leader wants to spend time with his wife and new baby, but a senior manager schedules meetings that begin at 6:00 p.m.
- *Interest in the industry.* Often college graduates take jobs that are the only ones they can get or because they sound interesting from the outside. Many find the industry to be boring over time. For example, a graduate may take a marketing job for an insurance company and realize that she is bored after five years of developing brochures for whole-life products. Or a supervisor in a manufacturing plant may get tired of monitoring the performance of a production line day after day. Personality, background, experiences, and culture all influence our levels of interest in specific industries. Sometimes they just do not fit.
- *Personalities of people in an organization.* Years ago, I was working with six executives who ran a division of a larger company. Five were introverts and the sixth was an extrovert. He nearly lost his mind working with the others. When the company grew, he would probably have hired others who were more like him, but I would guess that he left before that happened. Certain types of people seem to thrive in specific organizations and others do not make it. Usually, the personality of the organization is set by the founders, who then continue to hire the same type of person over time. I did training for a company about fifteen years ago and during the program we measured personality. Ninety percent of the eighty-five managers who participated in the management development program had the identical personality

type. That type is found in only about 1 percent of the population. That result is not a coincidence. An individual who does not have the same personality type will probably leave eventually. Ironically, in this example, the CEO of the company had a different personality type and, within five years, he "retired" at the urging of the board of directors.

There are, of course, other reasons why effective leaders leave organizations regardless of their level. This would include personal reasons like a spouse wanting to relocate, a child's allergies, schools in the area, cost of living, and family problems. We have very little control over these issues and it is best to leave them alone. Too often, we try to intervene in family situations during the selection stage. For example, when a candidate's spouse does not like the location of the company, it is common for the company to offer extra incentives, bring the spouse to the city for an expensive visit, and find friendly people to say good things to the spouse about the city. This can backfire later if the spouse's reasons for not liking the move come to fruition. It can also lead to marital problems. If a candidate or spouse does not like the location of the company, there is little that a hiring organization can do about it. If you talk such a candidate into taking the job, you will be lucky to keep that person a few years.

By the way, during the selection interview, it is appropriate to ask a question like this: "Is there any personal or professional reason that you would not be willing or able to move to [insert the name of the location]?" If they say no, follow up by saying, "We do not want to make an offer and find out that your spouse or significant other is unwilling to live here. If you find that is the case, please let us know."

Guidelines for Retaining Good Leaders

For purposes of helping you retain good leaders, I focus on what we can control. The items are listed in the same order as in the previous section and provide guidelines for retaining good leaders.

Money

As mentioned previously, money is not the primary motivator of most leaders—power is. Although they may not admit it, many would take a pay cut to have a leadership position. As an example, most government leaders in Congress could earn substantially more at other jobs. Many leaders are motivated to serve others or to work for a cause about which they care a great deal. Some people are independently wealthy and do not need a paycheck. Money will not be the reason that people like this leave leadership positions. That being said, most of the rest of us work for a living. If leaders are making their living by working in their leadership positions, money does matter. How much is enough?

The amount of money that we must pay a leader to stay depends on a number of variables including average earnings in comparable positions, location, type of position, pay policy, and management philosophy.

AVERAGE EARNINGS FOR OTHER LEADERS IN COMPARABLE POSITIONS

Companies should participate in salary surveys (a human resources professional should be able to obtain copies of these or conduct a survey) and monitor the environment. Salary information is also available on the Web now at many different sites. It is important because there will be interaction between leaders in similar industries and organizations. They will become friends and colleagues. They will visit each others' offices and homes. People notice how much money others appear to have, and they compare themselves. If a leader believes that a comparable leader in another organization is making substantially more money, the leader will be more likely to leave.

REGION WHERE THE ORGANIZATION IS LOCATED

Organizations can pay less in cities and parts of the country where the cost of living is lower. Salary comparisons should always be made within a specific region. Comparisons of salaries between small rural areas and major metropolitan communities are generally worthless.

If an organization is located in a remote rural area that is perceived as unattractive and people who have the necessary qualifications for the leadership position are currently living in large cities, pay will have to compensate for the location. In other words, to get a potential leader to relocate to the rural area, a company may have to pay more than the leader would make in a large city. This will be negotiated when the job offer is made. Any successful organization that chooses to remain in an unattractive area will have to cope with this disadvantage in order to recruit the best leaders.

TYPE OF LEADERSHIP POSITION

For example, sales management positions tend to pay more than operations management positions. Positions that require specific technical expertise tend to pay more than those that do not. The more training and education required, the more the position must pay.

PAY POLICY OF THE ORGANIZATION

Most companies have a match policy. This means that they want to match the pay of other organizations to be competitive. A few companies, on the other hand, have "lead" or "employer-of-choice" pay policies. In these cases, the companies have decided that they want to pay slightly more or substantially more in order to stand out from other organizations. The hope is that they will be the first choice of the best-qualified candidates for leadership positions and that they will not lose good leaders down the road. If everything else is in place, these types of policies certainly will not hurt them.

MANAGEMENT PHILOSOPHY OF THE ORGANIZATION

Many years ago, a CEO told me that he changed his mind about whom to promote to a senior-level position. He did so because when he first talked about the position to the internal candidate, the candidate (a manager with an excellent performance record) asked what the pay would be in the new position. The CEO was offended that the candidate seemed more interested in the money than the job. Perhaps the CEO overreacted to the request for salary information and maybe he did not. His philosophy was that the work should matter the most to his executives. To some that sounds naive, but he was the boss and got to make that decision in the company he ran. On the other hand, he lost a very good leader to a competitor.

There is another consideration in regard to pay. Research suggests that top performers, as strong leaders are apt to be, prefer individual rewards. Many companies have started to use group incentive programs because they tend to have a positive effect on the average worker and the bottom line. However, an excellent worker may feel that he or she is carrying the rest of the group and may leave because of that. For example, a sales manager whose territory consistently outperforms other territories should receive commissions and bonuses related to her unit's performance aside from the company-wide profit-sharing plan. It is important to continue to provide individual recognition and rewards to the best workers in our organizations.

To summarize, money usually is not the most important reason that a leader leaves, but combined with other areas of dissatisfaction, it matters. My recommendation to organizations is to constantly monitor the external environment on pay and make sure that leadership compensation is at or slightly above that of the competitors.

Advancement and Achievement

The opportunity to advance one's career or to achieve a goal is the most likely reason for a leader to leave one organization for another. Strong, effective leaders seek opportunities to lead. When they master one position, they look for a new one. The simple explanation is that this is their nature or inclination. The personality traits and life experiences that make individuals effective leaders also make them ambitious. This ambition may be geared toward personal achievement and advancement or it may focus on the achievement of a community goal or the advancement of a cause. Any way you look at it, to keep strong leaders, you must challenge them. They are very unlikely to reach a point where they are satisfied to vegetate in one position.

Approaches for keeping leaders' needs for advancement and achievement filled vary depending on the size of the organization. I address both separately.

ADVANCEMENT IN A LARGE ORGANIZATION

Years ago, almost all large companies used internal labor markets. That means that they hired only at the entry level and promoted from within. In a large organization with many promotional opportunities, strong leaders should be encouraged to apply for jobs at the next level. In these types of companies, employees may have 50 to 100 pay grades to work through, which will keep the most ambitious people busy for their entire career. A friend was recently promoted to regional president with a Fortune 500 company. When asked how many others there were with her job title, she said about twenty-five. Few companies have twenty-five "presidents."

In addition to promotions, strong leaders can be given extra assignments and projects. Whenever possible, these should be work related, but heading the United Way campaign is an excellent way to develop leadership skills, introduce leaders to executives and others in the organization, and provide visibility to community leaders. Note that not even strong leaders will be successful at every assignment they are given. The experience that they gain and mistakes made on less important projects will be valuable later when every project will matter. Leaders who are motivated by power will have a need to meet other organizational leaders and interact with them. Bosses should include them in meetings with executives and groom them to make presentations to executives and board members.

Strong leaders should be encouraged to go back to school. If they do not have an appropriate master's degree for their industry, they should be urged to pursue one. If they have a terminal degree for their field, they can take additional courses, participate in professional association conferences, earn professional designations like Chartered Life Underwriter (CLU) or Certified Employee Benefit Specialist (CEBS), and attend development seminars. One of the best ways to learn material is to teach it. If a leader has a particular strength, ask the person to teach it to a group of other managers. Developing leaders tells them that you care whether they are successful and builds loyalty. Even if they do not stay with the organization, they will remember who helped them advance their careers.

It is important to note that many organizations have turned away from an internal labor market approach because of competition. They need minds that develop outside of the company as well. It could also be that American workers have turned away from internal labor markets because of layoffs and a growing attitude that companies are not loyal to them. People are more apt to change careers and jobs several times over a lifetime than at any other time in history. This means that companies no longer have a guaranteed pool of qualified people to fill leadership roles. Therefore, keeping them is important.

ADVANCEMENT IN A SMALL ORGANIZATION

In small organizations, it is more difficult to promote strong leaders because there are fewer levels and positions. Typically, there are fewer turnovers in executive positions in smaller organizations, but that varies by location and industry. The bottom line is that there are fewer promotional opportunities, and managers have to work harder to keep strong leaders motivated. The traditional achievement ladder is not as visible.

All of the development strategies listed above for large companies are available to small companies too. Tuition assistance is important. In addition, leaders should be encouraged to participate actively in professional associations and particularly in leadership roles. A small organization can encourage a leader to run for an officer position with a professional association, provide time off and cover travel costs for meetings, and even provide some support for the association in the form of office space and administrative support. This gives the leader an outlet for ambition, more practice leading, and more external contacts.

Sometimes it is possible to create new departments and positions for particularly promising leaders. If the strong leader can develop a new service or cost savings, it may be worth it in the long run to create a job for someone who is bored in the current position and would be likely to leave otherwise. Few small organizations can do this for everyone or do it repeatedly, but it might be better than losing someone for whom a position will be available in a few years.

Another effective strategy might be to outline a succession plan for a small company that will show strong leaders where they will be if they stay. One example of how this would work was reported in the media. Jay Leno announced his retirement—in five years. Simultaneously, NBC told Conan O'Brien that he will be given the job as host of *The Tonight Show* when Leno retires. This was done to keep O'Brien in the family, so to speak. It is an unusual thing to hear about publicly, but small organizations can do the same thing. Not only will it provide motivation for strong leaders to stay, but it gives the parties clear-cut guidance on the development activities that are necessary.

Strange as this may sound, small company executives may want to help strong leaders find jobs outside their organization. Although it is unlikely they would return, the company would have a potential recruit for a high-level position later on, would earn loyalty toward the former boss and employer in future business dealings, and could earn a reputation as an organization that develops strong leaders. It is common in midsized cities to have one or two small companies that use this strategy and get lots of business from the ex-managers whom they have helped move up and out. It is also common for the ex-managers to return to fill executive positions later.

Problems with the Current Position

One of the most common reasons for strong leaders to leave is because of problems they encounter in the organization. The sooner that the problems are detected, the sooner they can be solved. Years ago, I was hired by an extremely vindictive director who resented any manager reporting to him who had been hired by the previous director. He gave them poor reviews, spoke disrespectfully to them in staff meetings, and held them to higher performance standards than other managers. In addition, he began planting seeds of doubt about their performance with senior-level executives. As a result, all of the managers, which included some top-notch professionals, left the company. I and some of the managers who were hired to replace the previous managers observed what happened and, eventually, all of us left the company too. This is a problem that could have been detected by senior management, but it was not and it cost the company. A number of things can be done to avoid problems that lead to turnover of strong leaders.

First, executives should constantly scan the environment for problems. There are a number of indicators that there might be leadership problems, which include the following:

- High turnover by workers in a department or among managers
- Many disciplinary actions being taken by managers
- Turnover in a department that is unusual for the company
- An increase in grievances filed
- A drop in unit performance on measures like productivity, sales, quality, or accident rate

Let me clarify that by managers, I am referring to individuals who hold management positions in organizations. They may or may not be leaders.

It is important to observe new managers to detect problems and to provide guidance. Managers are generally not given any supervision of their management or leadership skills. Executives tend to look at unit performance and make assumptions about their leadership skills. Certainly, if their unit's performance drops, that would be an indication that their leadership skills may be lacking, but it could also mean that there are other problems like a lack of resources, a downturn in the business, or the loss of a productive worker through no fault of the manager. Managers (to return to the distinction between managers and leaders made at the end of chapter 1) may try to please their bosses, even if it includes compromising their own values. Leaders who encounter these kinds of problems, on the other hand, are less likely to complain or to kiss up to the boss. If the situation cannot be improved, they either try to overthrow the boss or they leave. I have seen it work both ways. Both outcomes are bad for the boss.

The management philosophy must be continuously articulated and, more important, modeled by senior-level managers. When managers do not practice the management philosophy, the organization needs to get rid of them. They have a negative impact on all other members of the organization and provide poor examples for future leaders. Giving up on a manager who does not deal with others the way the organization wants is doing the right thing.

There are a number of ways to find out about the morale of the organization. One scientific approach is through an attitude survey. Hire an outside firm to conduct the survey and make sure that it is done anonymously. The results of the survey can provide a benchmark for improving the work environment that will produce more effective leaders and encourage them to stay.

Critical incidents should be studied as well. Unusual problems or situations that occur can tell leaders a great deal about the work environment and the quality of leadership in the organization. I worked in a company where one of the middle managers was accused of a very unusual type of sexual harassment by an employee. We did not learn of the behavior until the employee shared it during an exit interview—this employee quit because of the behavior and was going to a competitor. We investigated and found out that one of our senior executives knew of this manager's previous arrest record for similar behavior and never told anyone. The incident in our company might not have happened if that executive had been a real leader. In addition, we found an unusually high number of turnovers had occurred in the manager's department. Besides that, we found that the manager had promoted a worker to a supervisory position even though the worker had a history of excessive absenteeism. Those issues should have been investigated earlier by the manager's director and the head of human resources. We lacked leadership in several areas of the company, which was exposed because of this very unpleasant situation. These kinds of situations result in strong, effective leaders questioning the values, strength, and common sense of their colleagues. Several good people left this organization shortly after this occurred. They did not leave because of this specific incident, but rather because of a pattern of problem situations that suggested an environment of poor leadership. Executives should take an inventory of the problems that have occurred and understand the message being sent. The CEO may not be aware of everything that goes on in a company, but many employees often are.

Executives must fix poor performance. Performance should be measured, benchmarked, and monitored over time. People need feedback. We fix poor performance with feedback, training, mentoring, coaching, rewards, and disciplinary action. To keep strong leaders, they must see that performance matters. Few things turn off a strong leader more than sloppy performance as the standard in an organization. Even a few poor performers who keep their jobs or get rewarded in spite of it will discourage the best employees, whether they have leadership roles or not. Performance must be valued.

Lower-level leaders must be empowered to make change. Critical problem incidents and poor performance occur in all organizations. Leaders who are empowered to do something about it are more apt to stay. This should be done gradually over time. If a newly appointed supervisor finds a performance problem with a production worker and is empowered, he may provide some coaching to fix the problem. A supervisor who is not empowered will feel frustrated and may give up. If a director of public relations is empowered to address a difficult situation with the press, without clearing her statements with the CEO, she will feel as if she is trusted and capable. She is more likely to stay.

It is critical that resources are provided to leaders when they are assigned new projects. Budgets should be adjusted to meet the needs of the expected outcomes. It is very common among companies that provide consulting assistance to clients to knowingly submit bids that are far below actual costs to get a contract. I have heard two examples from two people in different Fortune 500 companies recently. Both individuals work for firms that provide consulting services to important organizations. Their companies submitted low bids and are now delivering slipshod (in one case, it was described as worthless) work because the budgets for the projects are not close to covering the costs of doing the jobs correctly—their executives will not let them spend adequate funds to do the job correctly and they cannot raise the budgets. In both cases, I asked these professionals if the team that developed the budget deliberately submitted wrong numbers to win the contract. The answer was yes. One of these people is a strong leader and will leave his organization soon. The other is not a leader, is bound by golden handcuffs (i.e., her pay and benefits are so high that she cannot afford to change jobs and maintain her current lifestyle), and plans to retire soon. She will stay—with very low motivation. In both cases, everyone loses. Some readers might be thinking that if successful companies are doing this, why shouldn't they do it too? Eventually, these companies will fail.

Senior executives must make working conditions as good as possible. It may be impossible to change the amount of travel that a leader has to do, but it is possible to allow her to invite a spouse or friend to go on a trip to a nice location and spend a few extra days on the company tab. It may be unavoidable that the plant is 100 degrees in the summer, but it is possible to provide cold bottled water and chilled snacks for free to the workers. It may be inevitable that the parking lot is a long walk from the work entrance, but the sidewalks can be kept clear of snow and ice. Little things can affect strong leaders' perceptions of the organization and make them want to stay.

Note that in all of the advice given in this section about how to keep problems from driving away strong leaders, the executive team is teaching leadership. If we model it, it will come—to paraphrase a line from a popular movie.

Unmet Needs

When our needs are not met, we have a tendency to leave an organization. A variety of needs are met by our jobs or leadership positions: power, recognition, affiliation, prestige, friendship, income, benefits, interaction with people who share our interests, fun, and opportunities to work with equipment and expertise that we could not afford on our own (e.g., planes, laboratories, spaceships). If more executives would realize that employees and, in the case of the subject at hand, strong leaders have needs that are met by the nature of the work, turnover would be greatly reduced in all organizations. The rewards that come from organizational life can be immense.

What this means is that we can often keep strong leaders even when the pay is not so great by doing the following:

- Providing necessary resources
- Recognizing good work publicly and privately
- Giving more freedom to those who earn it
- Allowing and encouraging cohesiveness and teamwork
- Making sure that benefits are equivalent to those in comparable organizations
- Organizing social activities and encouraging participation—maybe even on company time
- Following through on promises
- Making sure that equipment and supplies are up-to-date and working

These are small things in most organizations and relatively inexpensive, with the exception of benefits and equipment. Organizations that work to meet the needs of employees win the best leaders and followers.

Sometimes, unmet needs are personal and not within the control of the organization. For example, in some locations of the country, meeting another single person for a relationship may be difficult due to ethnic, religious, or racial differences. In some situations, medical reasons may force people to leave. Strong leaders may leave good organizations to meet personal needs. When this occurs, it may tell you that your realistic job previews should include realistic location previews too.

Much has been written about the number of well-educated women who are leaving fast-track careers when they have children. This development is puzzling to many people. *Fortune, Harvard Business Review,* and *60 Minutes* have had features on this issue. Although there are many theories, the women who are interviewed say that they left their jobs because they wanted to be with their children full time. I believe that we have to take that at face value despite recent research suggesting that women are also leaving in order to find more fulfilling work when their children are older. How many men would work outside the home if they had a spouse who provided a good income and material goods and if it was socially acceptable? If these women divorce, as 50 percent of Americans do these days, they will return to the workplace. Very few women both have successful careers and live up to traditional standards of housekeeping, marriage, and child rearing. More research and discussion is needed on this phenomenon. However, organizations will continue to lose promising women leaders if they decide to leave the workplace when they have children. By the way, it will continue to be inappropriate (and illegal if you hold the answer against her) to ask a woman in an interview if she is planning to have children.

Lack of Fit

We all have different preferences and interests. The insurance industry does not appeal to everyone. If an insurance company hires a top-notch vice president of strategic planning, he may leave because he does not want to spend his career talking about property and casualty policies. An automobile manufacturer may select a director of communications with a stellar background in the recording industry. He may do a terrific job for you, but leave because he misses the excitement of the music business. There is little that you can do about that except to maintain a positive relationship with this leader for the future. You never know when this individual may need insurance or a new car.

Besides industry preferences, sometimes there are management differences. One local company decided to hire only new managers with a military background. Several of these new hires came from the old school where they expected to give commands and to have employees obey without question. In an organization where everyone is taught to challenge the processes and policies in order to make quick organizational changes, this model did not work. By the same token, people who prefer a participative environment do not adapt well to authoritarian workplaces.

During the selection process, hiring managers must find ways to communicate well what the organization is about and the philosophy by which the company is managed. The following are some approaches to letting candidates for leadership positions know what they are getting into:

1. Critical incidents can be shared that illustrate the management values of the company. For example, during the interview process, talk about how the sales manager handled having to pull a top-selling drug from the market. Talk about what happened—even if it went badly—and how it fit or did not fit the company values.

2. Candidates can be shown a sales presentation on the company's products. They can be invited to try a product and visit the marketing and product development teams.

3. Candidates can be invited to visit with subordinates informally to discuss the work environment.

4. A very secure devil's advocate can be assigned to talk to candidates about negative aspects of the organization. Few people reading this book will ever actually do this, but if they did, they could avoid leadership turnover later. If the negatives are relatively few, candidates will be very impressed that they were given complete information up front. This is the type of thing that candidates should be told: "We expect our leaders to work until the job is done. If you need a forty-hour work week, you will not find it here." "You will have to travel two days per week. If that is a problem, this job isn't right for you."

It is important to note that needs change over time as leaders' personal lives and career goals shift. Executives should follow up with every strong leader to assess what may have changed. At least annually, a meeting should be held to determine whether there is a need to change the type of work being done by the leader, whether the difficulty of the work has gone up or down, how the leader feels about work colleagues, how the travel is affecting the leader's personal life, and what contacts the leader needs to make in order to develop. Meeting shifting needs is a bit more complicated but essential to retain strong leaders.

Examples of Leader Retention Strategies

Remember our six positions? Let's revisit them. Assume we filled each position with a strong and effective leader and that we were diligent about making sure that there was a good fit prior to selection. Brainstorm about some of the ways that we might be able to keep these leaders engaged in our organizations.

President of the Sunshine Fishing Club

Provide frequent informal recognition for the time and energy donated by the president. Give formal recognition at meetings at least once per year. This might include plaques, a special fishing rod, or another memento. Club members should talk with the president about new types of trips that will make the job more interesting—perhaps an international trip.

Vice President of Planning for a Fortune 500 Company

Provide frequent performance feedback to the leader. Provide access to all corporate stakeholders and communicate a high level of support for the planning function. Work with the executive team to implement strategic plans. Provide opportunities to interact with other executives in the community. Serve as an advocate for the vice president in all internal and external settings. Talk with the vice president about career plans. Few leaders want to do strategic planning for more than five to ten years.

High School Principal

The superintendent and the board members should visit the high school frequently and participate in the activities of the school. Provide frequent feedback on positive aspects related to the school and help solve the problems. Encourage the principal to continue to take courses and develop leadership skills. With strong principals, talk with them about moving up to becoming superintendents if they are ambitious. If there are no openings, assign challenging special projects. Look for innovation that might be implemented and involve the principal.

Director of Public Relations for a Historical Society

Encourage the director to participate actively in the professional associations and to take a leadership role. Provide opportunities to attend professional conferences. Involve the director in executive meetings and decision making. Use the director proactively, not just when there is a problem. Be open to new ideas and initiatives when the director returns from professional meetings. Look for internal opportunities to move up in the organization and provide training to broaden the director's skills.

MAYOR OF A MIDSIZED CITY IN THE RUST BELT

When a political party has a strong incumbent, members of the party should provide public support for the mayor and the administration's initiatives. Personal criticisms should be discussed and resolved outside of the media. I live in a small city where the mayor is continuously being criticized by members of his party who serve on city council. The public has the impression that it is personal. Although a thorough public discussion of all public issues is appropriate, personal animosities should be taken care of privately. Citizens and members of the party need to be careful not to give gifts or other favors that could be construed as a conflict of interest, but verbal messages of recognition and thanks are necessary. Effective public office holders should be encouraged and supported if they are willing to run for higher office.

CEO OF A LARGE URBAN HOSPITAL

CEOs get little recognition outside of the public flattery that goes on for political reasons. Boards and subordinates of strong, effective CEOs need to recognize their leadership skills. For board members, this can be done in board meetings and through raises. Subordinates have to be careful about creating the perception that they are trying to get something from their bosses (*brownnosing* is the common term), but it is appropriate to mention the CEO's significant accomplishments and changes and how they have helped a department. Make sure that CEOs see the good news—letters of appreciation from clients, improving sales figures, increasing efficiency measures, and positive comments from industry analysts. Even the best CEOs need to hear how valuable they are to their organizations in order to want to stay.

The retention of strong, effective leaders is a continuous challenge that is often left to fate or to paying leaders so much money that they cannot leave (the "golden handcuffs" mentioned earlier). I advocate a proactive approach whereby members of organizations work constantly to develop and retain the best and brightest leaders.

Selecting Government Leaders

The presidential election of 2004 was one of the most talked about in many years. The two candidates had distinctly different beliefs about leadership and both domestic and foreign policy. Voter registration and turnout were very strong. This highlights at the national level that people do care about those who lead them. Unfortunately, we rely on the small percentage of people who are willing and able to run for office.

Our fantasies about powerful people come from old stories about kings, queens, sheikhs, emperors, castles, jewels, gold, royal steeds, and palaces. These are all images of immense wealth, privilege, and protection from the rigors of ordinary life. Who wouldn't want to be a prince or princess? In these systems of government, individuals were born into their office. There was little discussion about who would be the next king. As we have seen recently with the British royalty, politics (not to mention sex) are still involved, but the line of succession is very clear. In earlier times, deposing a king or queen took a war, which was inevitably waged by someone with tremendous wealth. Think about the political campaigns that preceded those events.

In the United States today, our royalty are the president, vice president, senators, governors, or congressional representatives. Those titles do not have quite the same ring. In fact, the term *politician*, in general, stirs up negative attitudes. Additionally, being in charge is no longer necessary to live a relatively healthy and safe life. The bottom line is that few Americans are willing to make the sacrifice required to serve in a drab public office. Nonetheless, most of us are willing to complain about those who do. The objective of this chapter is to discuss ways to get the best and the brightest in our state and country to run for office.

Current Political Leaders

First, let's look at some recent and current leaders. Who are they? Where did they come from, and why did they run? If you examine the candidates for president in the last four presidential elections, you will find the following:

1992: George H. Bush. Son of a wealthy senator, attended Yale, military veteran, held numerous offices including senator and vice president prior to becoming president.
Bill Clinton. Son of a hairdresser, attended Georgetown University and Yale, was governor of Arkansas prior to being elected president.

1996: Bill Clinton.
Bob Dole. Midwestern war hero, served as a senator before running for president, son of the manager of a creamery and a sewing instructor, served in the military during World War II and was injured in Italy, attended law school at Washburn Municipal University.

2000: Al Gore. Son of a wealthy senator, attended Harvard and served in the military, served in the Senate and as vice president before running for president.
George W. Bush. Son of a wealthy president, attended Yale and Harvard, served as governor of Texas before running for president.

2004: George W. Bush
John Kerry. Son of a wealthy family, attended Yale and Boston College, served as a senator before running for president.

Obviously, much more is known about each of these men, but look at the common threads. All were educated at elite institutions that serve a small and highly intelligent group of students. Most came from families of wealth and power. Although we know some demographic information about each man, we will never know all of the reasons why they ran for president. Each would say that he wanted to serve the country. That is probably true for all of them. However, there are other motives, which may include the following:

- Pressure from family—most of these candidates came from families in which holding public office is a tradition.
- A need for power—it is unlikely that anyone who runs for president is lacking a need for power, because the presidency of the United States is the ultimate power trip.
- A need to prove oneself—men who grow up in successful families have hard acts to follow and earning the presidency is a fine way to show that you lived up to the family name.
- Financial gain—although presidents do not make much money, they earn substantial speaking and book fees after they leave the presidency.
- A desire to achieve a social goal or to right a wrong.
- Inspired by a significant role model—both Clinton and Kerry claim to have been motivated to seek public office by President Kennedy.

Encouraging the Best and the Brightest to Run for Public Office

The most important issue for the American public, or at least that segment of it that cares about the future leadership of the country, is how we can get more and better people interested in serving in office. Too many people claim to be voting for the lesser of two evils. Too many people complain about the lack of choices among candidates. Too few of us are willing to run for office ourselves, however.

A few years ago, I attended a dinner to thank our legislators. Most of the honorees were friendly and competent, if not well qualified, but several were not. It was scary to meet some of the people who control the policies, budgets, and laws in my community.

We have talked about the reasons that people might run for the highest offices in the United States, but we also need to talk about why so many people do not run. Here are a few of the reasons and some suggestions for changing the picture.

Reason 1. Little encouragement from family and friends to run for public office. Without any empirical evidence to back this assumption, I think it would be safe to say that most of my friends and colleagues would discourage their competent children from running for offices where they could impact the lives of millions of people. None of them, however, would discourage their competent children from becoming doctors, lawyers, or engineers.

We must provide motivational and financial support to children and friends who indicate an interest in public service. We need to create, find, and engage children at early ages in activities that encourage them to want to lead in government. We must direct them toward institutions that will train them for public service.

Reason 2. A lack of universities training people for public office. Although our senators and congressional representatives have attended many different universities, there are common patterns which suggest that attending Yale or Harvard gives one an edge, at least in winning the presidency. Many colleges have a political science major, which often leads to law school, which sometimes leads to running for public office.

More universities, maybe all of them, need to have courses and majors geared to training students for public service. A required course on public service would make a good option for a general education curriculum. It might also ensure better funding of higher education by governments. In early courses, the best and brightest students should be encouraged to become involved in majors and courses that will educate them for public service instead of being pushed into fields perceived as more lucrative. That takes us to reason 3.

Reason 3. The best and the brightest make more money working in business and other professions while controlling smaller budgets and affecting fewer lives than their counterparts in government do. Most businesses base their compensation on the scope and requirements for each job. They understand that to attract the top applicants, an organization must pay comparable wages. Government offices should pay wages comparable to those of other professional occupations. The compensation must take into account any requirements to maintain two homes, one in the home area and one in the capital city. Paying government officials well may even reduce government corruption. That takes us to reason 4.

Reason 4. The perception of politicians is often very negative. This makes sense when you consider the recent political campaigns for president. Unfortunately, research suggests that voters respond to negative advertising. It appears that the candidates need to run each other down and in some cases exaggerate in order to win. Of course, there are also horror stories about corrupt government officials. Just one story can color the attitudes of the public about all politicians.

This is a tough reason to overcome, but the public needs to begin viewing politicians or government officials as professionals. They should be elected based on their professional qualifications as well as their ideology. Voters and the media need to focus on attributes like whether they do their homework, whether they understand the issues, whether they correctly represent the views of the voters in their area, and how effective they are, or will be, at passing legislation, instead of discussing their behavior as twenty-year-olds.

How can we get voters to change their method of assessment of candidates? This is a classic question of which comes first, the chicken or the egg. The structure of governments must change, the quality of candidates must improve, and the public must adjust their attitudes. The media can help, but professional qualifications do not make good press. For example, newspapers can focus less on an errant comment made by a candidate during a speech and more on past performances and credentials when discussing candidates. Schools can also help. For example, in civics classes we can teach less about bureaucracies (which also turns off young people) and more about qualifications for elected office.

Reason 5. There are too many low-level government officials, which makes for fewer qualified individuals and a dilution of financial resources. Given the low number of people willing to serve in public office, the more positions there are to fill, the more difficult it becomes to find qualified candidates. In Erie, Pennsylvania, an economic expert has recommended that local city and county governments consolidate their functions. This would save money, improve the quality of leadership, and make marketing the community to expanding companies more efficient and effective. This is a trend in local government and would improve leadership tremendously. Local political hacks could be retired and ambitious, energetic professionals could move into well-defined leadership positions.

More local governments should consider merging and consolidating their functions. Current administrations can lay the groundwork for these kinds of efficiencies on their way out the door and make a significant and lasting contribution to their communities.

Reason 6. Running for public office may require giving up one's personal life and privacy. Certainly, investment in property contingent on a publicly funded development project should be made public, but the names of people a candidate dated and a spouse's treatment for depression are not.

The press and opponents should stop reporting that type of old news and the public should stop reading and listening to it. In the past ten years, one highly respected public figure refused to run for office despite wide encouragement to do so, specifically because his wife did not want to give up her privacy. We lost a potentially effective leader. Only the public can change this pattern.

Reason 7. Ideological compromises appear to be required to successfully run for office. Traditionally, this may have been true, but we have seen notable exceptions. John McCain and Arnold Schwarzenegger diverge from their party's lines frequently and it has served to make them more popular.

Voters want candidates who think. The major political parties will disappear if they do not allow candidates the flexibility to truly represent the voters. Americans may fall into red or blue states, but we all grew up believing in the same things. We may have different attitudes about how we achieve our goals, but the goals are the same. More politicians need to remember that.

Reason 8. Many Americans distrust government. The origins of this distrust are probably rooted in our history, in particular the independent nature of the American farmer. We are afraid of slippery slopes that could lead to loss of freedoms and rights. Some of us believe that every law passed represents one less privilege to choose.

While working on a phone bank for a candidate during the 2004 presidential campaign, several people told me, "They are both liars." Americans just do not trust government leaders. The cause of the negative perceptions of politicians does not always come from real incidents, but rather from films like *Dave* and *No Way Out*. People tend to see popular films and television shows and believe that those kinds of things go on all the time.

Changing this perception would be tantamount to changing human behavior. The more outrageous and scandalous the behavior, the more attention we pay and the longer we remember it. Again, as the quality of government leaders improves, the image will change and people will learn to trust them. This will take time and it will not happen on its own. As it changes, more of us will become willing to be part of that profession.

Reason 9. Holding public office is seen as either a job for those who cannot get another or a luxury that only the wealthy can afford. The entrance of wealthy men from other professions into politics demonstrates this. Historically, lawyers have made an easy transition to politics (e.g., John Edwards), but recently we are also seeing physicians (e.g., Bill Frist) and actors (e.g., Arnold Schwarzenegger) running for office. Many of the best and the brightest do not consider public office a viable option unless they are already financially secure.

We must begin viewing public office holders as professionals who have chosen to do this job for a living. As people begin to consider holding public office as an appropriate way to make a living, the quality of candidates who will "apply" will improve.

Choosing the Best Leaders for Public Office

Every four years, we have the opportunity to vote for president of the United State. Every six years, we elect or reelect our senators. Every two years, we elect or reelect members of the House of Representatives. Along the way, we elect all of the officials in other public offices. How can we make better decisions about which candidate will do the best job? We cannot put the candidates through a comprehensive screening as we do if they apply for a job with our organization. However, there are a number of things that we can do.

First, request and demand accurate and concise "resumes." It is fair for voters to ask every candidate to provide the same information that we would ask of a job candidate—after all, that is what they are. This resume should include the following:

- *Education*—degrees, institutions, majors, minors, dates of completion
- *Work experience*—names of organizations, job titles, descriptions of job duties, dates of employment
- *Military service*—branch of service, dates of service, job title, responsibilities
- *Community service*—names of organizations, dates of service, offices held, responsibilities, purpose of the organization

- *Special skills*—such as public speaking skills, leadership skills, budgeting, and financial management, including information on how the skill was acquired

Personal information should not be included in the resume. A candidate's spouse, children, and parents should not be relevant when we decide how to vote. Interestingly, voters weigh this type of personal information very strongly, sometimes more than actual qualifications.

Second, voters should insist on town meeting formats that allow them to ask questions. Currently, candidates make up their own schedules and formats for their meetings with voters. When voters insist on asking questions or they will not show up at campaign-controlled meetings, candidates will begin to give them what they want. Think of how much money would be saved if only a handful of meetings and debates were scheduled one month prior to each election and all of the meetings and debates were televised. Think how much more we would learn about candidates if the questions being asked did not have to be screened by each candidate's campaign committee first.

Third, voters should consider the office very carefully and decide which attributes are most important to the leadership position. For example, the president is the commander in chief of our military forces. Should military experience be required? The president must meet foreign leaders. Should the president be multilingual? The president must travel continuously. Should the president be an experienced traveler? The president must make many speeches. Should the president be an excellent public speaker?

Unfortunately, we tend to focus more on attributes like whether the candidate is a "good guy" rather than whether the candidate is qualified for the office. The candidate being a hunter (or not) should be irrelevant until the president is required to bag a deer in order to feed Americans. Sometimes, people still think in terms of prehistoric times when the leader of a group of humans needed to be a big, strong guy to personally fight off the saber-toothed tiger to protect his tribe. Maybe the tendency to vote for the taller, stronger-looking man is instinctual behavior on our part.

Instead, the voters should list the attributes that are actually needed. The following is a sample of attributes that I consider essential for the president of the United States, along with a measure or way of knowing whether a candidate has the attribute.

1. *Intelligence:* May be indicated by the level of education and choice of vocabulary.
2. *Honesty:* May be indicated by previous personal and professional behavior.
3. *Social skills:* Will be seen in appearances, speeches, interactions with others that we can view.
4. *Presence:* When the candidate enters a room, do people notice?
5. *Speaking skills:* We can hear this.
6. *Able to handle difficult and confrontational situations well:* We can observe this during debates and during questioning by voters.
7. *A complete understanding of the law and a history of following the law:* Since the president is the top law enforcement official in the country, understanding the law is critical. In addition, any pattern of violating the law would be a bad sign. Minor infractions while under age twenty-one are probably not relevant, but that depends on the type of violation and how many people were or could have been affected.
8. *Military experience or expertise in some form:* As commander in chief, the president has to have a thorough understanding of how the military operates.
9. *Foreign experience:* The candidate should speak another language and have a well-rounded background on foreign cultures, have held a job in another country, or have extensive experience traveling to foreign countries.
10. *Successful previous work experience in a high-level office in the public sector:* It is not unreasonable to expect ten to fifteen years of experience. It is the presidency, after all!
11. *Leadership style:* This is an open question, as an authoritarian style works well for some in some situations and a participative style works best for others in different situations. I would prefer a president who can use both styles effectively when the situation calls for it.
12. *Strong political connections to experts on national and international issues:* The president must have contacts and connections with experts from the United States as well as other countries and must be able to recruit a competent staff.

Now it is your turn. What qualifications do you think are necessary for the president of the United States? List them below.

_____

_____

_____

_____

_____

_____

_____

_____

_____

_____

It is one thing to list qualifications, and quite another to know if a particular political candidate has them. We do not get to administer personality tests or structured interviews to these candidates. Nonetheless, we can observe them, review their backgrounds, see how they handle difficult situations, and talk or listen to people who know them. It is tough to turn off the pundits and look away during the political ads. The best-informed voters do their own homework and ignore superfluous information during a campaign. They set out to gather specific information and vote based on the qualifications that they have identified and the information that they have found.

As citizens, we can also identify people who have the traits that we are seeking in leaders and ask them to run for office. It may take years before strong leaders work their way up the ladder to an important public office, but it is worth it when they do. This is one advantage of being young—lots of time. If political parties begin finding and encouraging the best and brightest young men and women to run for office early, we can build an adequate supply of candidates for Congress and the presidency for many years to come.

Improving Organizations through Improved Leadership

This book has described a long and detailed process for recruiting, selecting, and retaining strong leaders. The process is tedious and time consuming. Let me summarize the steps:

1. Develop a description of the organization, organizational characteristics, and primary issues.
2. List and describe the desirable attributes for the leader. Weight those attributes based on their importance to the job.
3. Recruit aggressively, using a specific strategy tailored to the position and the organization.
4. Develop a selection strategy that includes a variety of tools that will correctly assess the attributes that have been identified.
5. Sell the organization to the candidates.
6. Conduct screening using the tools that have been selected based on the required or desired attributes.
7. Compare the candidates.
8. Select the right person for the leadership position.
9. Socialize the new leader to the organization.
10. Provide training to develop necessary skills.
11. Address issues that could lead to leader turnover.
12. Follow up regularly to make sure that the match between leader and organization is still good.

I believe in leadership. Leaders matter. Sometimes we become frustrated by corporate or political scandals and begin to feel that we cannot trust leaders. Sometimes we truly cannot trust leaders. That does not mean that we have to give up. It means we have to work harder to recruit, select, and retain the best ones. Khurana suggests that many organizational boards are seeking "corporate saviors," CEOs who have done well in other organizations or industries.[1] As he points out, this approach does not work because it is based on the false belief that leadership is more about charisma than specific skills and knowledge. That is not true, and Khurana provides a great deal of evidence to prove his point.

The most effective leaders are not necessarily the best and brightest people, but rather the individuals who have the qualifications necessary for the roles that we need them to play in our organizations. The potential benefits are tremendous. What can we reasonably expect when we make good choices? Let's review the sample positions that we have been discussing throughout this book and talk very specifically about the outcomes that we could gain if great leaders are found. Then the reader can decide whether effective recruiting, selection, and retention are worth the time and energy that they take.

President of the Sunshine Fishing Club

1. More fun on the trips
2. Less money spent on the trips
3. Increased membership
4. Few problems on the trips
5. Less conflict among club members

Vice President of Planning for a Fortune 500 Company

1. Enhanced profitability of the company
2. Improved goal setting
3. Employees who understand what they are expected to accomplish and how their work affects the long-term goals of the organization
4. A strategy that is grounded in a strategic vision rather than limited by trends or weaknesses of the organization

5. A coordinated approach to implementation of the strategy
6. Positive attitudes across the organization about both the strategy and the plan
7. A strategy that fits the community and its priorities, needs, and opportunities

High School Principal

1. Better standardized test scores
2. Increased parental support
3. Increased community involvement
4. Fewer teachers' union problems and grievances
5. Improved support for funding issues on the ballot
6. Fewer disciplinary problems
7. Increased school satisfaction among students
8. More successful music, athletic, and other extracurricular programs
9. A more positive educational environment
10. Fewer students lost to private schools
11. Safer schools

Director of Public Relations for a Historical Society

1. Improved public perceptions of the historical society in the community
2. More support from legislators and other funding agencies
3. Better educational opportunities for citizens in the community
4. Advanced understanding of the history and heritage of the region
5. Increased attractiveness to scholars
6. Increased assistance to community leaders who market the region to prospective new businesses
7. Prevent public relations disasters from occurring

Mayor of a Midsized City in the Rust Belt

1. Increased safety in the city
2. Increased voter and business support for community initiatives

3. More businesses creating jobs and moving to the city
4. The city becoming a better place to live
5. Diminished brain drain
6. A tax base that increases, instead of decreasing
7. Increased civic projects
8. Improved appearance of the city
9. Retention of large employers and better companies
10. Increased pride of citizens in their city
11. Increased desire of competent people to run for public office
12. Decreased poverty and homelessness
13. Decreased cost of public services
14. Decreased taxes
15. Fewer problems with firefighters' and police officers' unions

CEO of a Large Urban Hospital

1. Increased number of people cured of their illnesses and injuries
2. Improvement in quality of doctors at the hospital
3. Increased community funding
4. Improved hospital efficiency
5. Decreased costs
6. Achievement of national ranking in the hospital's specialties
7. Prevention of nursing shortages at the hospital
8. Decreased turnover
9. Increased ability to meet community needs
10. Implementation of new approaches to serving uninsured patients
11. Improved health for the entire community through educational efforts of the organization

Your Position

How about your organization and the position you want to fill? What outcomes might you expect if you found the right leader?

1. _____
2. _____

3. _____

4. _____

5. _____

6. _____

7. _____

8. _____

You may think these outcomes are optimistic at best and unrealistic at worst. Not really. I could name numerous leaders who have achieved these kinds of results through their efforts. You could too, but you may not believe that your organization can ever find that kind of leader. You can.

Students in my interviewing skills seminars frequently comment on how much hard work selection is when it is done correctly. It seems discouraging to busy people who want to get it over with and hurry through the process. Some seem to be discouraged because they do not believe in leadership—that is, they do not believe that they can do better. I look at it as an investment of time. Sometimes I ask seminar participants to list all the bad things that have occurred when they made bad hiring decisions. The lists are very long, unfortunately. Of course, the bottom line is this: Wouldn't you rather have an effective leader?

The other problem is that many of us believe that we are good judges of people. We believe that we know a good leader when we see one. Most of us tend to hire individuals who look, act, and think like we do. This is not necessarily a conceited thing to do, although it can be. People who are like us make us feel more comfortable. If our organization is stuck in a rut, needs innovation, and requires change, we must find and select leaders who are different.

Finding the right leader can transform an organization. It is worth it!

Notes

Chapter 1

1. W. Bennis and B. Nanus, *Leaders: The Strategies for Taking Charge* (New York: Harper and Row, 1985).

Chapter 2

1. W. Bennis, *On Becoming a Leader* (Reading, MA: Addison-Wesley, 1989).

2. G. Yukl, *Leadership in Organizations*, 5th ed. (Upper Saddle River, NJ: Prentice Hall, 2002).

3. R. M. Stogdill, *Handbook of Leadership: A Survey of the Literature* (New York: Free Press, 1974).

4. D. C. McClelland, *Human Motivation* (Glenview, IL: Scott Foresman, 1985).

5. B. M. Bass, *Handbook of Leadership: A Survey of Theory and Research* (New York: Free Press, 1990).

6. A. Howard and D. W. Bray, *Managerial Lives in Transition: Advancing Age and Changing Times* (New York: Guilford, 1988).

7. C. J. Cox and C. L. Cooper, *High Flyers: An Anatomy of Managerial Success* (Oxford: Basil Blackwell, 1989).

8. J. B. Rotter, "Generalized Expectancies for Internal Versus External Control of Reinforcement," *Psychological Monographs* 80 (1966): 609.

9. Yukl, *Leadership in Organizations*.

10. E. A. Fleishman, "The Description of Supervisory Behavior," *Personnel Psychology* 37 (1953): 1–6.

11. D. Katz, N. Maccoby, and N. Morse, *Productivity, Supervision, and Morale in an Office Situation* (Ann Arbor, MI: Institute for Social Research, 1950); R. Likert, *New Patterns of Management* (New York: McGraw-Hill, 1961).

12. Yukl, *Leadership in Organizations*.

13. V. H. Vroom and P. W. Yetton, *Leadership and Decision Making* (Pittsburgh: University of Pittsburgh Press, 1973); V. H. Vroom and A. G. Jago, *The New Leadership: Managing Participation in Organizations* (Englewood Cliffs, NJ: Prentice Hall, 1988).

14. B. M. Bass and B. J. Avolio, "Developing Transformational Leadership: 1992 and Beyond," *Journal of European Industrial Training* 14 (1990): 21–27.

15. J. M. Kouzes and B. Z. Posner, *The Leadership Challenge: How to Keep Getting Extraordinary Things Done in Organizations*, 2nd ed. (San Francisco: Jossey-Bass, 1995).

16. S. Kerr and J. M. Jermier, "Substitutes for Leadership: Their Meaning and Measurement," *Organizational Behavior and Human Performance* 22 (1978): 375–403.

17. Yukl, *Leadership in Organizations*.

Chapter 5

1. H. G. Heneman and J. A. Judge, *Staffing Organizations* (New York: McGraw-Hill/Irwin, 2003).

Chapter 6

1. M. A. Campion, D. K. Palmer, and J. E. Campion, "A Review of Structure in the Selection Interview," *Personnel Psychology* 50 (1997): 655–702.

Chapter 9

1. P. Thoms, *Driven by Time: Time Orientation and Leadership* (Westport, CT: Praeger, 2004).

Chapter 12

1. R. Khurana, *Searching for a Corporate Savior: The Irrational Quest for Charismatic CEOs* (Princeton, NJ: Princeton University Press, 2002).

Index

Achievement, 141–42, 147; need for, 11

Advancement, 141–42, 147; in large organizations, 147–48; in small organizations, 149–50

Ambiguity, ability to deal with, 96–97

Analytical skills, 26

Appearance, 24

Assistant manager experience, 28

Attitude(s), 91; about value of organization's work, 95–96; toward aspects of business, 85–86; toward others, 28

Authenticity, 25

Authoritarian style of leadership, 29

Bona fide occupational qualification (BFOQ), 70, 121

Bush, George H. W., 160

Bush, George W., 160

Business knowledge, 23, 26

Calmness, 26

Candidates, rating and comparing. See under Leadership attributes

CEO(s): meeting current staff, 129–30; recruiting, 48–49; traits and skills needed by, 15; vision (see Vision, organizational). See also Hospital CEO; Salaries; specific topics

Cleanliness, 28

Clinton, Bill, 160

Club president. See Fishing club president

Cognitive skills, 11

Colleges, continuing education programs through, 135

Commitment, willingness to make long-term, 24–25

Communication skills, 24

Computer skills, 27

Concurrent validity, 61

Conferences, recruiting at, 46

Conscientiousness, 26, 78–79

Consideration behavior, 12, 28, 93–94

Construct validity, 61–62

Content validity, 60–61

Contingency theories of leadership, 9

Continuing education programs, 135. See also Training

Cooperativeness, 26
Creativity, 29, 98–99
Criterion-related validity, 61
Critical incidents, 151–52, 156

Demeanor, 24
Detail orientation, 92
Dole, Bob, 160

Education, 29, 134–35, 148;
  leadership, 14
Emotional stability, 11, 26, 80–81
Energy level, 11, 26
Engineering skills, 27
Expertise in field/industry, 23, 27
Extroversion, 26

Family orientation, 29, 90
Finances. *See* Money; Salaries
Fishing club president, 30, 37, 47,
  62–63, 157, 170; interview
  questions for prospective, 77–84;
  requirements and desired
  attributes of, 37–38, 50, 62–63,
  112
Friendliness, 26, 80
Frustration, ability to deal with, 28,
  96–97
Future orientation, 29

Gore, Al, 160
Government, distrust of, 164
Government employees, 163. *See also*
  Political leaders; Public office

Health and fitness, 29
High school principal, 32–33, 47–48,
  63, 157, 171; interview questions for
  prospective, 88–95; requirements
  and desired attributes of, 38–39, 51,
  63, 113–14
Hiring managers, 155. *See also*
  Recruiting; Selection
Honesty, 26, 77–78

Hospital: employees, 127–29;
  stakeholders, 127–29
Hospital CEO, 36, 48–49, 64–65, 158,
  172; interview questions for
  prospective, 104–6; requirements
  and desired attributes of, 40, 52,
  64–65, 116–17

Idealized influence, 13
Incentive programs, 146–47. *See also*
  Salaries
Individualized consideration, 13
Influence skills, 26, 97–98
Initiating structure behavior, 12
Initiative, 24, 29, 86–87
Inspirational motivation, 13
Integrity, 11
Intellectual stimulation, 13
Intelligence, 24, 29
Interpersonal skills, 11, 24, 29, 94–95.
  See also Relations-oriented behavior
Interviewing: research on, 75–76; tips
  on, 75–76
Interview questions, structured,
  69–71, 73–75, 144; closed- and
  open-ended, 68; examples of,
  68–69, 77–105
Interviews, structured, 67; guide to,
  67–74

Job offers, making, 121–23

Kerry, John, 160
Knowledge. *See* Expertise in field/
  industry

Language, 27
Law, knowledge of, 27
Leader behavior: categories of, 12;
  source of, 74–75
Leader(s): behaviors of good, 12–14
  (*see also* Leadership attributes);
  control, 142; determining what kind
  is needed, 2–4; lack of fit, 143–44,

155–56; positive outcomes gained
from selecting, 170–73; problems
with their position, 142, 150–53;
reasons for leaving, 140–44;
situational variables that affect,
14–19; traits of effective, 10–12,
140 (*see also* Leadership attributes);
types of, 2; unmet needs, 142–43,
153–55. *See also specific topics*
Leadership, poor, 142
Leadership attributes: assigning
weights to various, 111–17;
comparing ratings of various
candidates on, 119–21; identifying,
25 (*see also specific attributes*); rating
candidates on various, 117–20;
special abilities, traits, and
characteristics, 28–30, 38–40;
verifying the tangible required,
55–57. *See also* Interview questions,
structured, examples of; Leader(s)
Leadership experience, 28, 38–40, 84,
89–90
Leadership position: problems
with, 142, 150–53; selling the,
52–53
Leadership styles, 29
Leadership theories, 9
Learning ability, 23, 100

Management behaviors, 12–13
Management experience, 28, 38–40
Management philosophy, 130–32
Management preferences, 155. *See also*
Leader(s), lack of fit
Management trainee, 28
Managerial motivation, 11
Manager search, 21–25
Managers *vs.* leaders, 7, 151
Master's programs in specific fields,
134–35
Mayor, 35, 48, 64, 158, 171–72;
interview questions for prospective,
99–104; requirements and desired

attributes of, 39–40, 51–52, 64,
115–16
MBA (master of business
administration) programs, 134
McClelland, D. C., 11
Mechanical skills, 27
Meetings, recruiting at, 46
Mentoring, 136
Money: handling large sums of, 82–83.
See also Salaries
Morale of organization, 142, 151
Multiple-linkage model, 15
Multiple tasks in short time frames,
capacity to do, 24

Offers, making, 121–23
Optimism, 26, 79
Organizational age, 17
Organizational culture, 17–18
Organizational needs, 18–19
Organizational skills, 27, 99–100
Organizational vision. *See* Vision,
organizational
Organization(s): mission and business
of, 18, 125–26; problems, 16–17;
quality of followers, 18; size, 16; that
need leaders, scenarios of, 30–37;
types/categories of, 16
Organizing skills, 81–82

Participative leadership behavior, 12,
29, 87–88
Past orientation, 30
Performance data, willingness to
constantly monitor, 92–93
Persistence, 30, 102
Personalities of people in
organization, 143–44
Personality traits, 14, 24, 25–26,
37–40. *See also specific traits*
Personal life of leader, 143, 156,
163–64
Persuasion. *See* Influence skills
Pessimism, 26

Planning skills, 81–82. *See also* Vice president of planning
Political leaders, 159–60, 165; choosing the best, 165–68; current, 160–61; desired attributes of, 165–68; negative perception of, 162–63
Power, 144–45
Predictive validity, 61
Presence, 23
Present orientation, 30
President: of United States, 159 (*see also* Political leaders; Public office). *See also* Fishing club president
Privacy: giving up, 163–64. *See also* Personal life of leader
Professional organizations, training through, 135
Public office: encouraging the best and brightest to run for, 161–65; ideological compromises required to run for, 164; qualifications for, 165–68; reasons for not running for, 161–65. *See also* Political leaders
Public relations director for historical society, 34, 48, 63–64, 130, 157–58, 171; interview questions for prospective, 95–99; requirements and desired attributes of, 39, 51, 64, 114–15, 120

Rating system, 118. *See also under* Leadership attributes
Recruiting, internal, 53; advantages, 53; disadvantages, 53–54
Recruiting leaders, 43–44; contacting and screening potential candidates, 49–52, 54; locating potential candidates, 45–49; from other organizations, 45–46; selling the leadership position, 52–53
Relations-oriented behavior, 12. *See also* Interpersonal skills

Resources, sufficient *vs.* insufficient, 142, 152–53
Retaining effective leaders, 139–40; guidelines for, 144–58; and leaders' reasons for leaving (*see under* Leader(s))
Retention strategies, leader: examples of, 156–58
Rewards, 146–47. *See also* Salaries

Salaries, 141, 144–45; management philosophy of organization and, 146–47; of other leaders in comparable positions, 145; pay policy of organization and, 146; region where organization is located and, 145–46; type of leadership position and, 146
Sales skills, 24
Saltiness, 26, 88–89
Selection, 76; importance of, 1–2, 5–6; problems and pitfalls in, 4; steps in, 2–3; why organizations haven't improved the process of, 6–7
Selection strategy, developing a, 57–65
Selection tools: choosing the right, 62–65; reliability, 62; validity, 60–62
Self-confidence, 11, 28, 102–3
Situational theories of leadership, 9
Skill development, 133–37
Skills training, 27
Staff, introducing new leader to current, 129–30
Stakeholders, goals of, 126–29
Stogdill, R. M., 10
Stress tolerance, 11

Task-oriented behavior, 12
Technical skills, 11, 26–27, 37–40
Tradition, respect for, 104–5

Training: leadership, 14; through professional organizations, 135. *See also* Education
Training companies, for-profit, 135–36
Training programs, in-house, 136–37
Transformational leaders, behaviors common to, 13
Transformational leadership, 2
Traveling and travel business, 83–84, 103–4

Universal theories of leadership, 9
Universities, 162; continuing education programs through, 135

Values, consistent *vs.* inconsistent, 29, 85, 143
Vice president of planning, 31, 47, 63, 130, 157, 170–171; interview questions for prospective, 85–88; requirements and desired attributes of, 38, 50–51, 63, 112–13
Vision, organizational, 132–33
Visionary leaders, 30, 101

Working conditions, 142
Writing skills, 27

About the Author

PEG THOMS is an Associate Professor of Management and Director of the MBA Program in the Black School of Business at Penn State-Erie. Recipient of the Walter F. Ulmer, Jr., Applied Research Award from the Center for Creative Leadership, she has numerous articles in journals such as the *Journal of Organizational Behavior* and *Human Resource Development Quarterly*. Coauthor of *Project Leadership from Theory to Practice* and author of *Driven by Time* (Praeger, 2003), she has done extensive consulting, leadership development, and training with many organizations in the public and private sectors.